# WHY?

## By

# James W. Nichols

ISBN: 0-7596-5724-6

This book is printed on acid free paper.

1stBooks - rev. 3/7/02

# EVER WONDER
## ABOUT

AURA'S
MOODS
DREAMS
WEATHER
FIRMAMENT
MAGNETISM
EVOLUTION
ELECTRICITY
REINCARNATION
FROZEN MAMMOTHS
BODILESS SOUL'S
PLANTS & ANIMALS
LIFE BEFORE ADAM
ANGEL'S & DEMON'S
CONTINENTAL DRIFT
ENITY'S & SPIRIT'S
FRIEND OR ENEMY
CELESTIAL INFLUENCE
THE UNPARDONABLE SIN
YOUR FUTURE & YOUR PAST
OUR ORIGIN & WHY

**ME TOO, AND HERE
ARE THE ANSWERS**

This book I dedicate to my loving wife Phyllis who is the first person to Truly understand me.  I love her with all of my heart and could never have written or completed this book without her encouragement and help.


The dream of this book began way back in 1957 and has been floating in my mind till its completion in 1994.  Then I made a few minor changes to help with the readers understanding in 1996.

**James W. Nichols**
Author

Tucson, Arizona

# WHY?

# LIFE-ASTROLOGY-BIBLE

All of my life I have been asking, "Why?" In my young years many of my conversations with Mom and Dad ended up as, "Why?" When I went to school the main questions were, "Why?" Sometimes the why was just my antagonistic nature, most especially in the teen ages. Teachers got very tired of my raised hand in class, because they knew the question I would ask, "Why?" Well, it has taken 64 years for me to finally stop asking, "Why?" I would like to tell you about it as I think many of you wonder about the same things I have, and would like some straight and direct answers as I have.

To my questions very educated people have said "YOU MUST HAVE FAITH." Well, I do have faith and it tells me, if I ask for the truth, I will get it. Not always from the educated people of earth, you must go higher for good answers.

There are some very educated people who have almost come up with the answers, but they always seem to stop short of the complete explanation of, why. Hearing Oprah talk with author M. Scott Peck on July 14, 1993, was the straw that broke the camels back and resulted in the completion of this book. Mr. Peck comes so close to the truth and is so right in his thinking, but never finishes the total explanation that covers our smallest cell to our larger solar system.

As I served in the military during Korea, I heard reference, "It's best that the troops not be made aware. What they don't know, won't hurt them and it may keep them from being injured."

It seems that all of our lives we are in the dark for our own good by those who are all knowing. Congress feels that we should not know about this or that, so it's made confidential.

The government keeps secrets from us for our own good. I feel it's the upper class of people, maintaining control over the lower class. Being a part of the lower class, its time we stopped hiding the truth. Here comes the truth. I hope you can handle it, and I hope the U.S. Government leaves it in the book stores where you can find it. The government will take some books off the shelves. Yes, that is true. Just try to find a copy of "WE ALMOST LOST DETROIT" by John G. Fuller, published in 1975. The U.S. Government removed it off the shelves in less than two weeks. I knew about the book ahead of time and got one of the first copies. It is the true story of the FIRST NUCLEAR POWER PLANT ACCIDENT COMPLETELY CONCEALED IN 1966. The U.S. Government estimated in 1966 a Nuclear accident would result in 3400 killed 43000 injured $ 7 million in damages. They estimated contamination of an area the size of Pennsylvania. Still, they allowed the building of Enrico Fermi One. After the Fermi One accident the government revised the figures on their estimate to be 102,000 KILLED 610,000 INJURIES 40,000 CANCER DEATHS $ 314 BILLION IN DAMAGES.

This is what they learned from Enrico Fermi One after that 1966 accident. All you ever hear about is THREE MILE ISLAND. Will we never know about the **BIG SECRET OF 1966**, the ENRICO FERMI Melt down?

Yes, that is right! I just skimmed out of high school. I have never gone to college. I have no degrees from higher education except two degrees in electronics. All of my life I have read. I have almost gone broke buying book's several times in my life.

2

At one time had an entire multiple car garage full of books, while the cars sat outside. Today I have a very modest group of books in a very modest room. My mind is at rest in the truth I now know. I hope you may also find this rest.

Now that these things are clear, and you are fully aware of my back ground, I wish to share my hard earned answers with everyone who reads to find out why.

I ask why about my Mothers early death at 46 years. In my years as a child my Mother was a steadfast, solid as a rock person. My Dad and I counter on her every hour of the day. Always right there with wonderful and correct advice. Everything my Mother did made sense, except when she had a dream one night. All of our questions about her dream fell on deaf ears. It was not for discussion. The effect on Mom was one of confusion to Dad and me. Mother's frustration lasted about a week. We had never seen Mom like this before.

With time, the dream forgotten, life went on. Then one hot summer day I was working in the heat of the Sun on Mom's garden. She called me to the shade for some cold lemon aid. After cooling down, Mom asks me to use her old bellows camera and take her picture. The camera had always been off limits in fear of damage to the bellows. In shock, I ask why did she want a picture. She simple replied "You might enjoy the picture someday." Boy was she right. I look at it everyday. This picture turned out to be the only recent picture we had of Mom, Taken only a year before her death. She died in a car accident. Her life left her body at 2:00 A.M. I watched helplessly, as a teenage boy.

When we could manage to enter our old farm house in two or three days, we found vital papers already signed which relieved my Dad of all legal requirements. Our Christmas and birthday present with cards were in our store room. Mother put them there for Dad and me prior to her death.

My mother fed every animal that came near the farm. All 20 or so cats, 4 or 5 dogs were no where around after she died. Mother's prize rose's were all dead. Mother's famous can goods in our basement all spoiled. First loss of can goods ever remembered to spoil of Mother's. All of these things happened within the three or four days after her death.

Two years went by. My Dad and I had a visitor. It was a minister from the local town. He was leaving for another state and wanted to share some interesting information with us. It seems Mother had talked to him about her dream of dying. He said, "Over a year she knew she would die in an auto accident." She saw the whole thing in her dream with details that no one knew about except Dad and myself. Numerous details not in any newspapers. The news in those days didn't headline death and auto accidents as it would today. There was only a couple of lines in the COLUMBUS DISPATCH. It sure makes a lasting impression when it happens to someone you know so well.

A few years ago I found Mom's birth certificate. Born 10-12-1900 at 2 A.M. I had watched my Mother die 10-12-46 at 2:00 A.M. along the lonely highway.

I watched a doctor on TV today who said "Dreams, are not prophetic! Don't worry about them." Strange since history has detailed dreams of prophet's down the ages. Well, maybe your brain does clear out problems in dreams, but don't think there are not important vital messages when you need to know the truth, that come via dreams. History has proved this time and time again.

In the last ten years I have written small condensed articles and given them to friends. Some said "I just can't believe all that," or "I didn't have the time to read it." A few friends and my daughter Beah in Phoenix said, "Boy that makes the best sense, you should write a book." Well here it is BEAH. I had to wait for the proper time when more people were asking "Why?" Nobody knows about cycles better than I. That is what life is all about. Read Ecclesiastes the 3$^{rd}$ Chapter, Verses 1 to 9. There is a time and place for all things. **THEY ARE EVEN LISTED FOR YOU!**

Be advised I am **NOT A BIBLE PUSHER**. You do what you feel you should, but the Bible is the greatest history book ever written. We can learn a lot form it, all of us!

I'm sure there is a universal being in charge. There is to much organization in the solar system for no one to be in charge. A friend once said "The big bang theory is like shredding the phone book! Throwing it in the air, and having it come down in total order again! It just can't happen friends. Think about it! Someone is in control and you can call him or her, **GOD, JEHOVAH, FATHER, LORD, JESUS**, but someone is in charge. In this book I will call this **being** the Universal Intelligence or GOD, or UI. This **being** is better than any manmade computer even the 486's, and he has a direct line to every living thing on earth. **Animal, plant, tree, people**, are all connected. This line is like a wire and carries our electrical potential that we know as **life, spirit, holy spirit, aura**. It's the soul that powers our bodies. This power I will call an **Entity**. Without this power our body is a corpse. Remember I said our **bodies**, not our thinking. Our thinking or Entity lives on forever no matter what happens to our bodies. Our **ENTITIES** will live forever.

Inside a female the body parts assemble. She is the hot house for our seed to grow in. The spirit God supplies. With no electric spirit power to supply the Entity in the body, the body becomes just a dead body.

Being an electrical type Entity in these bodies of ours, we are therefore subject to changes in any electrical fields around us. Every thing is subject to fundamental electrical laws and formulas. Medical science is just now starting to realize this and is using electrical coils to increase healing of bones, magnetic resonance imaging, etc. The same thing done in 1967 resulted in jail for one man in Columbus, Ohio. The United States accepts Acupuncture today. China has used acupuncture for thousands of years. Acupuncture is the redirecting of body currents. The needle short circuits electrical systems of our body. We can also cause changes in other people that are near to us.

We are like our very planet and magnets. SEE MY **FIGURE ONE**. We are constantly soaking up electric waves or giving them out. That is the real reason we like or dislike other people. We feel their fields of electric around their bodies called AURAS. Magnetism draws us to others or pushes us away just like magnets. Of course there are many other considerations involved, but generally this causes a person look at someone and state "Boy oh Boy is he or she ugly." Other people may see them as very pretty. **REMEMBER**, "Beauty is in the eyes of the beholder!" Each aura gives off a FLUX FIELD. Some are strong, and some are weak. That is how the **HONEST** healers work. They use their AURAS WHICH IS A STRONG GIFT FROM GOD. Notice I said honest healers. There will always be fakes in everything.

Many things go into making up our AURAS or electrical fluxes or entities. How we look our ages, what cycle of growth we are in. These things are not just a matter of fact all of your life time. At birth the body design is a certain range of flux. This will govern who travels toward you and away from you. No one stays the same all during their life's. Some people change at 25, some at 35, more change at 38 to 45. The change of life syndrome is a fact. It happens to male and female! I have been in and out of it. It is a life challenger believe me.

6

# FIGURE 1

The Electrical magnetic field flux that extends from each of the earth's poles named the Van Allen Belts for the man who discovered them in 1700's. They extend out 40,000 miles from the earth and inner act with the Sun's radiation rays.

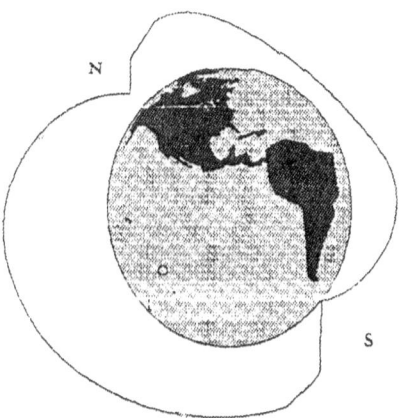

Humans, plants and animals have electrical magnetic fields just as the earth does. They are called Aura's and relate very much like the Aurora Borealis with colors and varied strenght. The Kirlian Theory proved this. Aura's relate to the electrical spirit within us and the moon effects them to cause our moods.

Bar magnets have the same type of flux fields as the earth and our aura's.

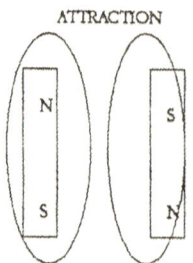

Humans, Plants, and Animal inner act the same way with their magnetic fields as bar magnets.

They attract or repulse between themselves according to their magnetic natures.

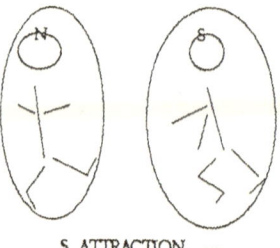

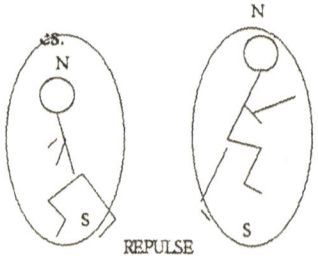

These changes turn into cycles in our lives. A baby that's beautiful at birth with good health, will cycle into poor health and a problem about high school time. Look at the kids on TV who were very popular in TV shows. Some then went down hill and into Jail, drugs, etc. Did you know kids in high school who were popular who went into life only to fail? Then there are those who were unpopular in high school who turned out to be a big success after school.

Everyone cycles from popular (positive) and unpopular (negative). Make a mental list of your high school friends and see if I am not correct. As I retype this, adding and deleting, the floods of 1993 are changing the lives of thousands of people around the Mississippi river. So many inner reactions are taking place. People helping others. People feeling sorry for themselves. People trying to steal from those losing everything. Those who could afford to help on vacation and not giving a damn. Plant closings, loss of employment, college people on the streets without work. Who determines who gets what and who does not? Well, in this book I will explain how it works, but every little step is important as you must "WEAR THE OTHER MANS SHOES TO KNOW HIS LIFE."

By now do you feel you may have wasted your money on this book? Well then let me give you a little demonstration. On the next page I have constructed a chart for you. It's composed of two disks you will put together yourself later on. This chart is for explanation only. Inside the small ring you have birth date, fun period, 4 poor hours, sympathetic, and bored. The next ring toward the outside has the months of the year with dates indicated. Locate November and then 25. I have set this birth date of November 25 for our demonstration. The outer ring shows the signs of the zodiac, Scorpio, Sagittarius, etc. Above these names are numbers such as o/30, 10, and 20. These numbers are indicators of the degrees of each of the zodiac signs.

9

Zero or 30 shows either 0 degrees of the beginning of a sign or 30 degrees at the end of a sign. To use

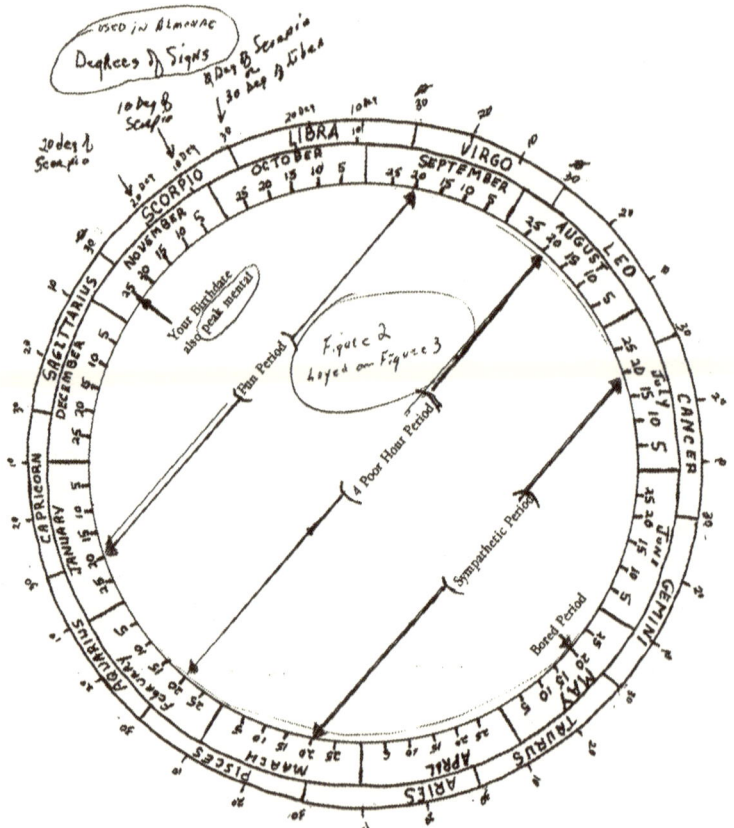

**Figure 5**

our example chart I have set the birth date arrow on 25 of November for a sample birthday. Note that this is just inside the sign of Sagittarius at about 2 or 3 degrees. This indicates where the Sun is on day 25 of November of any year. Please view that the **FUN PERIOD** runs from about 20 September to 20 January. The birth date arrow is to set our disk. It then becomes the **PEAK MENTAL PERIOD**. Please view also that the **SYMPATHETIC PERIOD** runs from about 20 March over to 20 July with the **BORED PERIOD** on 10 May. The last part of the chart indicates the **4 POOR HOUR PERIODS** at 20 February and 20 August. I have used the above dates to describe locations to you on the chart. We will now start to locate the degrees of the signs above these dates to use the chart properly. Note the following please:

| | |
|---|---|
| 25 November | is about 2 degrees of Sagittarius. |
| 20 January | is about 2 degrees of Aquarius. |
| 20 February | is about 2 degrees of Pisces. |
| 20 March | is about 28 degrees of Pisces. |
| 20 May | is about 28 degrees of Taurus. |
| 20 July | is about 28 degrees of Cancer. |
| 20 August | is about 25 degrees of Leo. |
| 20 September | is about 28 degrees of Virgo |

This chart works on the same basic principle as the Tides of the ocean. As the Moon travels around the outside degrees of each sign on this chart, each of us will experience these periods according to our birthday date and Sun sign. To find where the Moon is we will use the OLD FARMER'S ALMANAC. You can purchase one at any drug store in order to obtain up to date locations of the Moon. They generally cost about $4.75. For the purpose of my example chart I have written down 1993 July from the almanac for us to use. Please follow along as I explain the sample chart with the sample page from the almanac. Notice that each sign of the Zodiac has 30 degree's total.

The 25 November is 2 deg into Sagittarius. To find 2 deg of Sagittarius on our almanac of July 1993 look down the right side. The first Sag shows up on the 3$^{rd}$ or Saturday. Since there is three Sag's, this indicates the first is 0 to 10 deg, the second is 10 to 20, and the third is 20 to 30 deg. To locate 2 deg for this 25 Nov birth date the first SAG will cover this. You will note some signs show only two indicators while some show four. With 30 deg in each sign one indicator would show all 30 deg, while three would show 10 deg each. Four would show about 7 ½ deg for each indicator

Write down peak mental 3 July. With this example I will write down all of the other dates and signs as follows:

Peak--------------3 July 1993 Sat (2 deg Sag)

Follow to the left with me (opposite a clock)

Fun period-------6 July 1993 Tue (2 deg Aqu)
4 poor hours-----9 July 1993 Fri (2 deg Pis)
Sympathetic----11 July 1993 Sun (28 deg Pis)
Bored------------17 July 1993 Sat (28 deg Tau)
Sympathetic----20 July 1993 Tue (28 deg Can)
4 poor hours----23 July 1993 Fri (25 deg Leo)
Fun period------26 July 1993 Tue (28 deg Vir)

The example of July 1993 is as follows:

| Day of the month | Quarter Moon Place |
| --- | --- |
| 1. Thursday | SCO |
| 2. FR. | SCO |
| 3. SA | SAG |
| 4. SU | SAG |
| 5. MO | SAG |
| 6. TU | AQU |

| 7. WE | AQU |
|-------|-----|
| 8. TH | AQU |
| 9. FR | PSC |
| 10. SA | PSC |
| 11. SU | PSC |
| 12. MO | PSC |
| 13. TU | ARI |
| 14. WE | ARI |
| 15. TH | TAU |
| 16. FR | TAU |
| 17. SA | TAU |
| 18. SU | GEM |
| 19. MO | GEM |
| 20. TU | CAN |
| 21. WE | LEO |
| 22. TH | LEO |
| 23. FR | LEO |
| 24. SA | VIR |
| 25. SU | VIR |
| 26. MO | VIR |
| 27. TU | LIB |
| 28. WE | SCO |
| 29. TH | SCO |
| 30. FR | SAG |
| 31. SA | SAG |

The FUN PERIOD. It runs from the right, to the left of the top of the disk. It is the period of time when we are full of joy, playful, joking and feel good. The PEAK PERIOD is our top mental thinking. Our mind works at it's best now.

The 4 POOR HOUR period is the time when you drop everything, or get bad news. It's a time of worry or confusion, PMS in females. You lose things right under your nose. If you are asleep you can have bad nightmares. Upset stomach, headaches or insomnia, can slip right by you during the new moon period. The new moon is a sign of weakness in a mood. When the full moon is there it will be much worse and can jump the mood ahead by 24 hours if the full moon is close enough to your date of the 4 poor hours.

THE SYMPATHETIC PERIOD is when you cry for any small reason, or have a lump in your throat over a movie. Gifts mean twice as much now. Flowers just make the tears flow in females. Love and passion are very strong now and this is when the female's body temperature is high and they are very fertile to receive the seed of a baby.

THE BORED PERIOD is just that. Your attention span is short and you just can't stay interested in anything for any length of time.

If a sign appears more than once during the month, simply write it down with the date.

My sample month of July 1993 written down like the following allows us to see each month as it comes to us. Each month will be different, so check each one.

        Peak mental------------3 Jul 93
        End of fun period------6 Jul 93
        4 poor hours------------9 Jul 93
        sympathetic------------12 Jul 93
        bored-------------------17 Jul 93
        sympathetic------------20 Jul 93
        4 poor hours-----------23 Jul 93
        into fun-----------------26 Jul 93
        Peak mental-----------30 Jul 93

See my **FIGURE 12**. The new moon makes the mood very weak while the full moon makes the mood very strong and if a full moon is close to the 4 poor hour's periods it will jerk the date ahead by 24 hours. Check the dates for other NM and the FM and note where they happen.

Cut out FIGURE 2 AND THEN FIGURE 3. Lay them together as I did on my example chart. I trust that you were able to follow along on my dates so try your own now. Find your birth date. Put the peak arrow right at it. Read the outside ring of the outer disk for the approximate degree and sign and look them up in your active Almanac. The more months you follow it the more you will realize how correct it is and how great it is to see what mood your kids, husband, wife, mother in law, Mom, Dad, brothers, and sisters, are in.

You will find these dates need adjustment at first till you find the exact setting due to our different birth times, but it will answer a lot of questions about why people act one way one day, and another way the next day.

Why does it work? Well, that is a fair question. It works due to the same reason we have ocean tides. The oceans are salt water and the moon moves tidal waves as much as ten feet high around our planet. Salt water covers 2/3's of our globe. Until a few years ago science could not believe that the moon could do this when it moved around the planet, but science has finally given in and said that the tidal waves in oceans move with the moon. The full moon not considered as the cause of full moon madness by science, will learn like the police and hospitals. What few people realize is that the tidal waves move all over the earth from water to earth back to water and just keep going.

# Monthly Mood chart

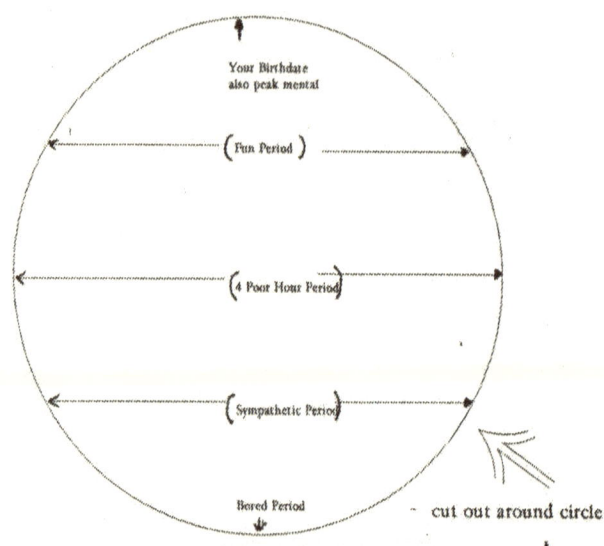

Your Birthdate
also peak mental

( Fun Period )

( 4 Poor Hour Period )

( Sympathetic Period )

Bored Period

cut out around circle

# Figure 2

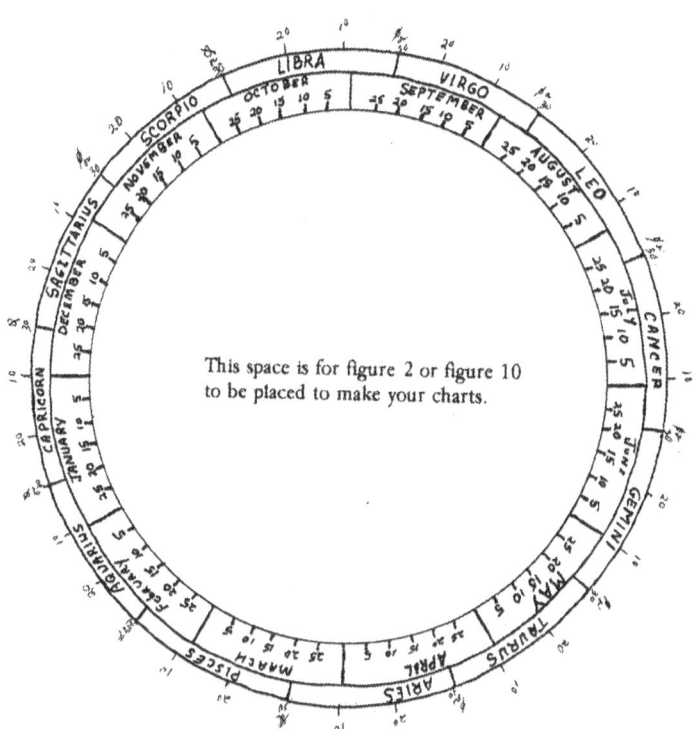

This space is for figure 2 or figure 10 to be placed to make your charts.

**FIGURE 3**

The New Moon is felt on earth as less light since it shields the earth from some of the Sun's rays during this time.

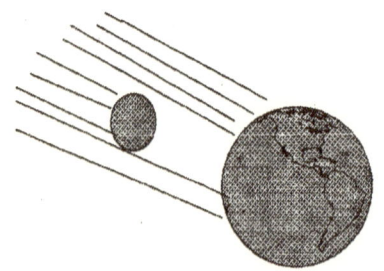

During the Full Moon period the earth receives light from the Sun in full strenght. The earth also receives light reflected by the Moon which increases the total rays considerably.

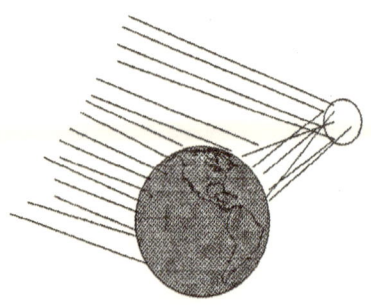

As the Moon leaves Full toward its half and quarter periods the Earth still receives full strenght from the Sun and lesser reflected light as the Moon moves between the earth and the Sun.

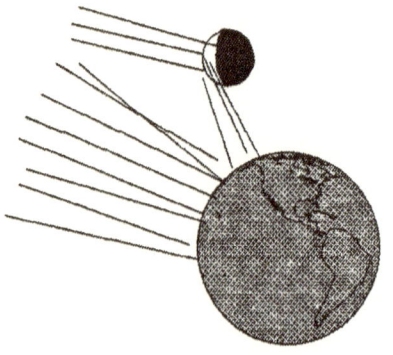

**FIGURE 12**

Science must now learn that human bodies, plants, trees and flowers also contain a living force that moves with these tidal waves down during the new moon and up during the full moon. In humans, who are almost two third's salt water, it reacts just like the salt water on our planet.

The reaction in people shows up as changes of our moods. That is why people are okay one day, and in left field the next. IT'S why people lose ball games one day and win ball games the next day. See my FIGURE 4 and FIGURE 6 to get an idea about tidal waves on the earth.

During the full moon hospitals try not to do operations because of the heavy blood flow during this period. Females during their periods flow more during the full moon too, so watch the date of the full moon each month.

This is how the almanac writers predict a year in advance the planting dates. The almanac weather was as good as the weather bureau until the writers of the almanac decided to use the sun spots as their guide instead of the moon. When to cut your hair for fast growth, and when to cut it for slow growth is in your almanac. This is why you cut your grass one time and IT'S up in almost 3 days. The next time you cut it, it takes 5 days to grow back.

This is how you know when to prune flowers, or trees, etc. There is a life force in living things, plants, flowers, trees that cycles up to the top and then down to the bottom into the roots. When the force is down into the roots you prune the top of the plant. The force then pushes the growth of the plant above ground. When the life force comes back up, it finds a smaller

19

# High tides pull where sun and Moon are while low tides are 90 degrees.

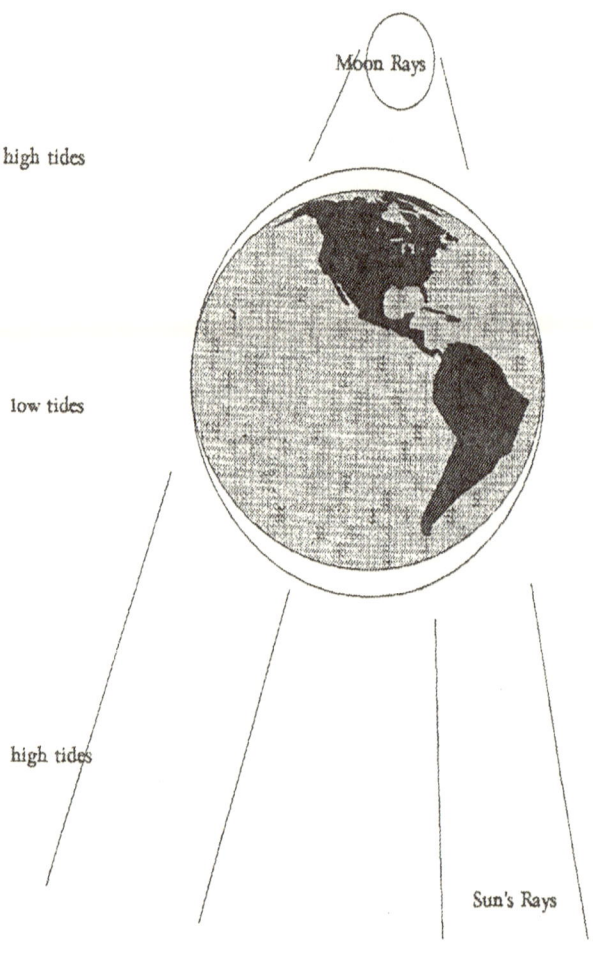

**FIGURE 4**

**AS THE MOON ROTATES AROUND THE EARTH THE TIDES OF EARTH SWING HIGH AND LOW <u>RELATED</u> TO THE SEASON OF THE YEAR AND THE SPEED OF THE MOONS ORBIT.**

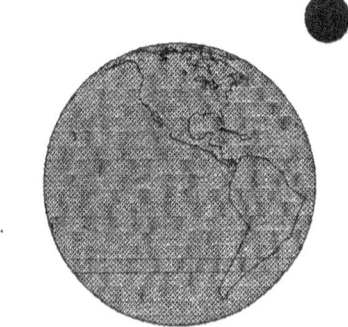

Spring bringshigh tides and fast orbit of the moon.

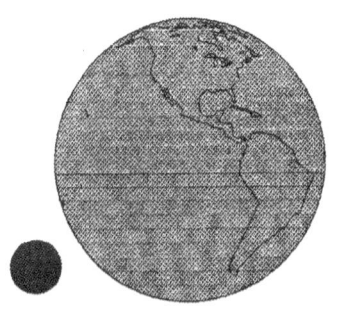

Winter brings low tides and a slow speed of the moon.

**FIGURE 6**

space to occupy than before. Therefore growth just leaps. That is what makes people with green thumbs. They know about this and follow the almanac. See the chart I have made for you below.

| | **New** | **1st Qtr** | **Full** | **Last Qtr** |
|---|---|---|---|---|
| Earth gravity | strong | weak | strong | weak |
| Blood Flow | light | | heavy | |
| Butcher meat | | best | | poor |
| Plant Seed's | above ground harvest | | below ground harvest | |
| Prun trees and plants | to stunt growth | | to increase growth | |
| Kill Weeds | | | best when moon is in Virgo Gemini Leo | |

**Figure 5**

Now in a garden some plants (like carrots) wish to develop under the ground, while others (flowers, tomatoes) like to develop above the ground. This is why there are dates for all things, even a time to kill weeds.

Well are you still reading? Is this book in a garage sale by now? I am about to start again. I will blow away your schooling and what the family has been teaching you.

Remember in high school about the continental drift? How the Ice age slowly moved over the planet? Well, if that is the case, how did engineers during WW2 find super large Mammoths in the Aleutian Islands QUICK FROZEN so fast they had food still in their mouths?

Every college library has a record of this fact with no answers for how it happened. Look up an author named Velikovsky. They don't believe him either, but read for yourself his feelings about the ice age. Well, let me tell you what I think happened. At one time our land mass was all on top of the globe while the water was all on the bottom. See my FIGURE 7.

The north and south poles were straight across. The weather was perfect up on the dry land. Dew formed on the land mass from the water on the bottom. The temperature was the same year around. The poles show no tilt as you would see them today. The first people arrived during this period of time. The people were perfect and the earth was perfect. What ever you and I think of as perfection, that is what was here for them.

This Universal Intelligence creates everything perfect according to the Bible so the planet was perfect, the weather was perfect and the people put here were perfect.

Everything was swell until one person got bored with perfection. **WOULDN'T YOU KNOW!** There will always be one person to screw up things. This guy

Estimated position of the Earth's Poles at time when the first people were placed into perfection.

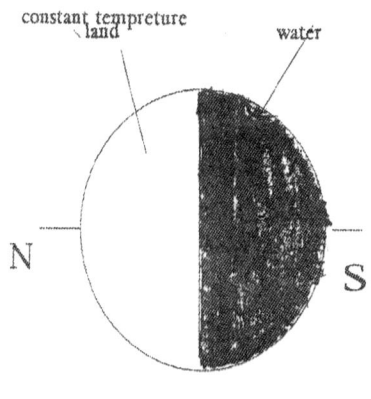

It was still in this position when Adam and eve were placed back on earth to populate for the second time and begin our schooling.

Earth after the continental drift caused the land seperation and froze the Mammoths in the Aleutian Islands.

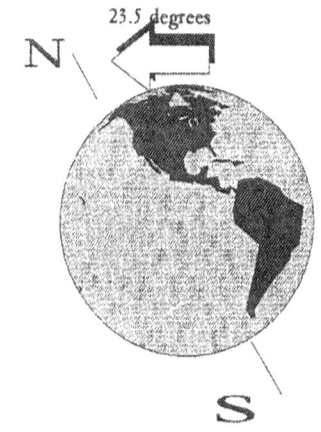

Read John White's Book on Pole Shift
1987 A.R.E. Press
P.O. Box 595
Virginia Beach, VA

**Figure 7**

who screwed things up was lucifer. You know, satan. All of this is in the Bible. It's debated by preachers every year. They don't feel you can handle the truth. This is why you don't hear ¼ of it. I would not say they covered it up, but they just have forgotten to tell you about it. lucifer (sorry I will not capitalize his name) talked his head off to all of the people and one third agreed with him and were willing to follow him in the need for excitement beyond paradise. The other two thirds walked away and said no. So 2/3's followed GOD'S wishes and 1/3 followed satan. satan wanted to take over heaven and control the planet to suit himself.

In this condition of perfection they could do anything they set their minds to, so GOD became forced to destroy by death all of their bodies. This left electric souls or entities with no bodies. Remember our talk about the spirit, AURAS, entities, corpses? This left the planet a mess with nothing but electrical entities or souls like static electricity, which is aware, know what is going on, can think, can sense, but have no body to enjoy sensation, touch or feel. They are in a fixed state of electrical static. They communicate by mental thinking but miss being able to talk from a body. This would be hard to give up now wouldn't it?

This is what lucifer achieved by talking $^1/_3$ of the people in to his dumb way of thinking. The two thirds who stuck by GOD are workers for GOD. Messengers to do his work and they are very happy, but the 1/3 are very sad, unhappy, and their souls have little to look forward to but boredom now.

Look at the BIBLE Genesis book 1, the second Verse, "AND THE EARTH WAS **WITHOUT FORM** AND **VOID** AND DARNKESS WAS UPON THE FACE OF THE DEEP AND THE SPIRIT OF GOD MOVED UPON THE FACE OF THE WATERS." Read it for yourself. Don't believe me. Read it for yourself.

This was the first screw up upon the planet.  It was before Adam and Eve.  Its name is the PRE-ADAMITE THEORY. Super scholars have talked about it for years, but will not discuss it with you, because you're not smart enough to understand about it.  I just happen to think we have the right to know and decide for ourselves.  Besides, with all of the evidence in the Bible they still fight with each other and against this thinking because then the end of the Bible would not scare you!  They have lied to all of us long enough.  This is as bad as Washington D.C. and the Government.  Some of the worst sinners in the world is so called religious people who have forgotten all about GOD and the gifts they have received from him.

JIM BAKKER went to jail for lying and cheating so many people, and all for the sake of money and high living.  He's out and back at it again thanks to the devil.

You must know that there are some honest preachers who are very good, mean well, with good wisdom, who try to help us all, but they too have left untold this story I have just given to you.  I think sometimes they don't even know the story.  The teaching of a preacher is, "**BELIEVE WHAT YOU ARE TOLD**."  My thinking is unpopular.  I found it hard to believe, but IT'S true and came from Bible studies from 1960"s on with only the Holy Spirit to guide me.

My only prayer has been for truth, and now that I have it, no one wishes to accept it.  Society directs all thinkings don't they? Well, read on or toss this book in the trash!  It could be your one chance to understand the real story of life and you have read a lot worse right?

I will name one preacher who teaches openly the pre-Adamite teachings.  His name is FINIS JENNINGS DAKE. He is not rich because he preaches the truth.  His Bible the "DAKE BIBLE" and is the best study Bible I have ever owned.  This

Bible contains more information in the columns on each page than I have ever seen before. It has information at the back of each book that tells you every detail of that book. In total IT'S the best reference study Bible made. It's not popular because preachers don't tell you about it. Stores don't carry it.

The address to order a DAKE BIBLE is DAKE BIBLE SALES P.O. BOX 1050 LAWRENCEVILLE GEORGIA 30046.

There are spirits in this world. Good spirits and evil spirits. There are two good spirits to every one evil spirit, so everything is in our favor. The good spirits came from the two thirds GOD chooses as his messengers. The evil spirits came from lucifer and the one third who followed him. The evil spirits are free to infiltrate any human spirit here on earth.

These spirits being an electrical Entity, and our spirit been an electrical Entity, they can interfere with our thinking, feelings, sensations, etc. They receive a gratification themselves through us and our bodies. GOD has provided two good spirits to fight on our behalf to ward off these evil ones. We only need to ask for the good spirits help and we will receive it. There is no excuse for our giving in to evil when help is as near by as our asking for it. Quietly and mentally! Just think (I NEED HELP)! No church setting required, and no preacher needed to help you. Wherever you maybe, THINK in your mind (GOD PLEASE HELP ME, I CAN'T DO IT ON MY OWN). Help is right there, just for the asking.

Connie Chung's program EYE TO EYE in October of 1993 showed people paying $ 1000.00 to get to use their Angels (or spirits). Isn't that sad. What GOD gave to us free of charge, we still feel we have to pay for it! Organized religion really has a hold on the world. Give your money and be saved. A Catholic Father interviewed on EYE TO EYE and his only reaction was, it was a joke, people paying for their Angels, but if he would have been receiving the money from sinners in a confessional, he would not have laughed. I noticed he did not mention the fathers who remove evil spirits for money all of the time. Don't they call it EXORCISM? It was first done in 1614.

What they do is ask two good spirits to remove the evil one because the Catholic Church knows about the real story I have just told you. It's noteworthy that most of the people with the need for Exorcisms are Catholics.

How are you doing so far? Has this answered a few questions for you? Did more questions pop up? It has helped me and I rest easy knowing I have two good helpers with me all of the time to fight off the one evil spirit when I am trying to write and tell you these truths. It gives me the courage to keep going despite the odds against truth in this world today.

Let's review shall we? Since lucifer and one third of the first people on earth screwed up and every one lost their bodies, GOD now realized people don't have the strength to handle the perfection and free will he wants to give to them. Our willpower is just not good enough. We always want more and more. With this in mind GOD remade the earth again as you read in Genesis 1, Verse 3.

This time, he had in mind to send entities in bodies to school to learn to handle perfection on their own. All of us, are now serving "ON THE JOB TRAINING" here on earth to be ready for the perfect heavenly life GOD wants us to someday have with him. We simply have to learn all of our lessons in this school by first hand experience. We must experience each and every trial and tribulation, joy, success, good health, ill health, and failure, personally, each of us. We cannot learn from others' mistakes, only from our own!

In Genesis 1, Verse 3 GOD made the light and divided it from day to night. I think **FIGURE 7** is a picture of the planet after the restored light. In Genesis 1, Verse 6 he makes the firmament. The original word is Cosmos. Cosmos means social system. He says the firmament is to divide the waters. I think IT'S to divide the old social system from the new social system he is about to start with Adam and Eve. That is how we came to have fossils' millions of years old. They are from the first social system that GOD destroyed. I don't believe these Mammoths or Dinosaurs were wild. They were part of the **perfect world prior** to Adam and Eve's world we now live in.

Genesis 1, Verse 14 has a special message for me. The lights of the firmament were for signs and for seasons and for days and for years. This would be the Sun, Moon and stars in our universe. He then Picks out two great lights in Verse 16 one for day (SUN) and one for the evening (MOON). Think about this. The Star's Sun and Moon are for SIGNS AND FOR SEASONS AND FOR DAYS AND FOR YEARS. This is the BLUE PRINT of GOD THE GREAT ARCHITECT. The firmament, made by GOD, showing his plan for all mankind. Ecclesiastes 3, Verses 1 to 8 indicates signs and seasons are:

"To everything there is a season, and a time to every purpose under the heaven. A time to be born, a time to die a time to plant, a time to pluck, a time to kill, a time to heal, a time to break down, a time to build up, a time to weep, a time to laugh, a time to mourn, a time to dance, a time to cast away stones, a time to gather stones, a time to embrace, a time to refrain from embracing, a time to get, a time to lose, a time to keep, a time to cast away, a time to rend, a time to sew, a time for silence, a time to speak, a time to love, a time to hate, a time of war, a time of peace."

That list is worth reading over many times. Then put them all into prospective in our history. This friend is only some of the handy work of GOD. Read Psalms 19 Verses 1 & 2.

To hopefully add fuel to the fire that is building inside you, read Genesis 1 Verse 28 where GOD said to ADAM AND EVE replenish the earth. Replenish in every dictionary means to fill again. This backs up the fact that Adam and Eve were the second group to be here on earth.

Look at Genesis Chapter 10 Verse 25 you will see that in the days of Shem (a generation of Noah's family) GOD DIVIDED the earth into continents, and islands. This division happened so fast, people moved **WITH**, the land mass they were on. There is no indication of loss of life. This would explain how the Indians were in America prior to Christopher Columbus. I also think the Mammoths quick frozen in the Aleutian Islands with grass in their mouths shows just how fast the continents separated and moved.

Suggested reading regarding this continental separation in one day's time is a book titled "WORLDS IN COLLISION" 1950 or "EARTH IN UPHEAVAL" 1955 by Dr. Velikovsky. "POLE SHIFT' 1980 by John White A.R.E. Press, P.O. Box 595 Virginia beach, Va.23451.

I must say Doctor Velikovsky was boycott by science, and his death was from disappointment of his peers. It is a very sad story. Notice when you add the BIBLE reading to his thinking, he makes excellent sense.

The height of the mountain ranges shows how hard the continents must have slammed together during this move. Science now agrees, that the continents moved from one piece of land. We then find the earth with continents as we see them on a map today, and oceans where also as we see them today.

SOME SUGGESTED READING YOU WILL FIND VERY INTERESTING FOLLOWS.

"THE 12$^{TH}$ PLANET"

"THE STAIRWAY TO HEAVEN"

"THE WARS OF GODS AND MEN"

"THE LOST REALMS"

"WHEN TIME BEGAN"

"GENESIS REVISITED"

ALL WRITTEN BY **ZECHARIA SITCHIN**

Sitchin, years in advance, pre-predicted many of the findings by the NASA voyager on other planets. He did this by his reading of the Sumerian Texts. **UNBELIEVABLE**.

We find the poles no longer straight up and down, but at 23.5 degrees tilted. The tilt of the poles could be the reason that the continents moved. It had to be fast due to the perfection of rock cuts made during this movement. The earth rotates at 1800 mph. That is very fast isn't it? Kelly's Island in Lake Erie shows some examples of the continental drift cuts. If the drift had been a slow movement, the cuts would have been uneven and imperfect as the earth moves imperfectly and with erratic movements. The cuts I have seen were clean cuts, and straight as a machinist would have cut them. A German scientist named Alfred Wegener proposed this theory. It's called the **PANGAEA THEORY**. The theory is that the dry lands you see on your globe at home are about 20 plates. These slowly float over magma and lava from the mantle inside the earth. Science has decided that the Himalayan Mountains were a result of India ramming into Asia and Europe. Fossil locations have backed up the floating plate theory. This theory of floating plate's sixty miles thick, science identifies as **PLATE TECTONICS**.

Near **Winslow Arizona** there is a super large meteor crater. It's ¾ MILES DIAMETER AND 620 FEET DEEP. That is large enough to have moved the poles of our earth from ninety degrees (straight across) to 23.5 degrees, where they are now. Did the planet earth get hit with something from outer space? We find two indentation's in the surface of the earth where the poles might have been once before. It's a fact, that the magnetic poles of the earth have changed polarization several times as indicated by the record of nature in our earth surface. Read Pole Shift by John White A.R.E. Press 1987.

Okay, back to our story. People spoke in different languages shortly after the PANGAEA because of trying to build the tower of Babel the Bible says. You can read about the confused language in Genesis Chapter 11.

Genesis Chapter one, Verse 20 God started creating a new set of animals. No, Dinosaurs or other strange animals dated over 70 million years ago. All of today's creatures of OUR HISTORIC PERIOD WERE MADE AT THE TIME OF ADAM AND EVE.

Genesis Chapter one verse 26 God put **MAN** in charge of all things. Would Adam have control over Dinosaurs? Was Adam 70 million years old or was Adam of another period of time? Dinosaurs lived in a period of perfection and lived with the first people of our earth 70 million years ago. Look at FIGURE 7 again.

Genesis Chapter one Verse 28 where God said to Adam **REPLENISH THE EARTH**. Funk & Wagnalls College Dictionary says, Replenish, fill again something wholly or partially emptied. Restock." This really tells it the way it is. Populate the earth again. Not like any Bible story you have ever heard before is it, because our teachers choose not to tell us, or perhaps they just don't know. Many conflicts throughout the Bible are no longer in conflict because we can now separate Adam's world and the world before Adam. Many prophetic statements are about the first world and not of the future at all, as most preachers tell us. OF COURSE HISTORY REPEATS ITSELF, so almost every preacher tells us about the prophecy of Isaiah for the future. Now we find out most of it was about the past too. We never knew that there had been a world prior to Adam. Now that will really change your outlook won't it. All of a sudden the Bible makes sense and has context. Conflicts become non-conflicting. We should have known. Man has always messed up everything he has ever touched, unless he had God's help and the help of the HOLY SPIRIT. Did you know one super intelligent person came up with the year system in the Bible? People of religion teach that anything prior to 4,000 years is not Bible right. One Roman Catholic Bishop proposed the time and date of the Bible stories. Did GOD put Adam and Eve on earth 4,000 years ago? We have had science giving us dates of Dinosaurs at 200 million years ago while the Bible teaches only 4,000 years. The Catholic's have much information they will not share with anyone because once again we can't handle it. Our brains are too small, or are our pocket books too small?

Review time........We start with Adam and Eve on a new rebuilt planet with all the land on the upper half and all the water on the lower half. The poles are straight up and down. The Sun is the same distance at all times therefore the temperature is constant. (See **FIGURE 7**). Adam has only one rule to live by to please GOD, just don't eat from this tree of good and evil (Genesis 2:17). What TYPE OF TREE is not necessary. It was just the first rule for Adam and Eve to follow. Genesis 3:6 Eve talks Adam into eating from the tree disregarding the one rule.

Sound like lucifer talking into her ear? Next we notice they are wearing clothes. That was the beginning of clothing stores, credit cards and the like. Only one rule and they broke it. Now, Eve and all females will endure pain in child birth Genesis 3:16. So ladies you can blame Eve for all of your problems, if it helps at all, plus men now know why there is PMS.

Just as a matter of information only, it's interesting to notice that Noah's sons who went on the Ark with him were Shem, Ham, and Japheth. In exploring the names you find that Ham means burned. Then Ham had four kids' one who was Cush. Cush means BLACK, so it looks as perhaps the black race started here. It really does not matter, but it's interesting! They found black people in other lands after the separation of the continents. Ever hear that before? The Indians were here in the USA when Columbus got here right?

Adam and Eve's kids progressed generations. The world had evolved to the stage of Sodom and Gomorra. Have you forgotten Sodom? In Sodom men wanted men more than they wanted females! Oh yes it's right there in Genesis Chapter 19 Verse 5. Two Angels came to Sodom and Lot went to meet them. He beds them down at his house for the night. Genesis 19:4 the men young and old circled the house and wanted the **NEW MEN** who came to town. In Genesis 19:8 Lot offered the men outside, his **VIRGIN** daughters. The men refused the daughters. These men are BLINDED to quite them down.

**THINK ABOUT IT! THE DESTRUCTION OF SODOM WAS BECAUSE OF THIS.** What will our fate be by allowing homosexuals to be open in our streets the way they are today? Bad news I think. Now I have lost all Homosexuals reading this book.

Back to our story line … Why was the world rebuild with Adam and Eve? When people could not handle paradise, the

Universal Intelligence felt we needed training to accept paradise. With proper training GOD could give us paradise, This is his desire and with training we would not disappoint him again. The result is a school on earth with the beginning of Adam and Eve. Now we can learn all the facts of life just as indicated in Ecclesiastes 3:1 to 9. With that list in those verses no one life time will allow us to experience all of these things. Therefore we must to be born over and over again. We finish one life time, die and are born into another life time. In a different setting each time, We can experience every single thing personally involved in earthly life. Birth, death, planting, reaping, weeping, laughing, mourning, dancing, casting away, gathering, embracing, refraining from embrace, to get, to lose, to keep, to cast away, to sew, to rend, silence, speak, love, hate, war and peace. That says it all doesn't it? WAS ANYTHING LEFT OUT? All of these things we must experience during our lifetimes down here on earth with our fellow men.

Remember the sayings we have heard all of our lives? "YOU CAN'T KNOW UNTIL YOU HAVE WORN THE OTHER MANS SHOES." This is really true. Until you have experienced it personally you can't know how it feels. After you experienced being burned you will avoid getting burned again won't you, because you remember how it hurt and you don't wish to have the pain again.

If you have been in jail, you try never to make that mistake again. Now I know you're saying, "What about the people who make the same errors for a full life time?" Well, they will return and be exposed over and over till they get it right.

Some people are born to push forward society and progress. This would update the schooling situation and, progress our lessons. The main object for us to learn is to love each other without any qualifications. We should learn to love nature, plants, animals, children, mothers, fathers, brothers, blacks, whites and on, and on! We're on earth by birth into an area where the lessons we need will take place. If we step outside that area into other areas we get hurt every time. It's like trying to skip a grade in school and jumping into another grade.

The one rule I have found that GOD has lain out, that disrupts our schooling down here, is SUICIDE. **THE UNPARDONABLE SIN**. That's the one thing that stops our education. We and only we decide to take our own lives. We are the only one's who can commit suicide. No one else can do it for us. Others may help and direct us, but it is totally of our doing and in my opinion it drops our souls out of the recycle schooling here on earth completely. We never get to recycle back to earth again. This is the one thing that sends us to satan's group of bodiless souls. Every lesson you can name will only result in our having to relearn that lesson again in this life or have to return to learn it over in another life. I hear some of you saying there are no reincarnation stories in our Bible. They tell you this, and you believe without reading yourself Matthew 17: 11, 12, 13. John the Baptist was Elijah returned. Jesus Christ said that himself. If you study your Bible you will find 14 similar points found between John and Elijah. Even more is written in 1 Kings 17:1, 2 Kings 2:11, so folks, the Bible presents no problem with reincarnation. ONLY PREACHERS HAVE TROUBLE WITH IT.

You can't name one of the ten commandments in Exodus chapter 20 that will send you to hell. Breaking them will cause you hell on earth, but will not send you to satan's bodiless souls. You may have to come back and learn over again not to break that law, but is satan's bodiless group your result? You simply broke a rule that requires additional education. If you read carefully you will see that Jesus will forgive you of anything, but not once did he forgive suicide.

Why are some people rich all of their lives? Why are some people poor all of their lives? Some are sick all of their lives and some are healthy all of their lives. Is this fair? No, it's not fair! When you look at each life as a group of lessons, with your soul returning to gain more lessons, then it's not so unfair is it? Everyday people are coming up with past lives they remember when under hypnosis.

People who know only English have been fluent in a foreign language under hypnosis. I know the medical people don't believe in it yet, but they are always behind. They don't like to stick out their precious reputations. On file and in documentation is the story of a young female 7 years old who expressed concern over her husband and children. The family finally took her to professional psychiatrists, one after another, until one psychiatrist took her to his friend a hypnotist and the hypnotist learned where the family was and their names. He wrote to them in another country. On validating their being real, and alive, at his own expense he traveled with this 7 year old to this country where he had found them. As the 7 year old got off the plane she saw them standing at the terminal. She went direct to them, called each by name, ask if they were okay, and the hypnotist and little girl returned on the next flight to the USA. The 7 year old never spoke of the family again. They solved her problem. She knew they were okay. Read some of the books written by people of education. TV will not tell it all for you. I have read about people afraid of water. They learned by hypnosis of being drowned in a past life. No longer were they afraid of water on earth. Read these books. Doctor Raymond A. Moody, Jr. MD. Book "LIFE AFTER LIFE," is very good. Doctor Cal Jung "The Tibetan Book of the Dead." Doctor Frederick Lenz Ph.D. "Lifetimes."

Another author and Doctor Elizabeth Kebler Ross instruct dying people to deal with death in a positive way. You don't see her on the evening news programs, but every nurse in the world has studied about her. She tells of a salesman that came on an accident in the highway. He stopped and talked to the woman who was dying from the accident. She begged him to find her mother in an Indian reservation. To tell her not to worry as Dads spirit was there with her, then she died. The salesman, impressed with her request, drove 300 miles out of his way to find this woman's mother. He told her what the daughter had said and the mother cried for several minutes. When composed she explained that the girl's father had died only a few minutes before the daughter's time of death. The daughter could not have known her father was dead.

Look at the children who appear in this world gifted in music, knowledge, etc. Where did they learn these things? Even TV told about the 12 year old who graduated from collage. He could have only carried this knowledge along with him into this life, from a past life. There is never any explanation about this from Doctors. They don't believe the reincarnation thinking. They have answers for everything else.

Have you heard of Edgar Cayce? You should read about him. He was just a regular person like you or me. He had very little money. He read the Bible everyday. With only a grade school education he spent most of his life helping others with his gift. He found his soul had the ability to leave his body, and move anywhere he desired. One time he saw the book of life with all of our names written in it. The Book of Souls name is THE AKASHIC RECORDS. Most of the time he left his body to visit other peoples souls. He found he could look into their souls and see imbalance or sickness. He also discovered his mind, with no training in the medical field, came up with cures to sickness. Just like witch doctors in the tribe's years ago that we heard about.

Tribal Witch Doctors used only herbs, tree bark, etc. They cured so many sicknesses. That's how Cayce worked. He had his wife sit by his body and he would transmit with his voice the cure for another person's body. People all over the world wrote to him and for no charge at all he would lie down, put himself into a trance like state of mind. His soul would travel to the sick person's location. In this state he could see the problem and then relate the cure to his wife. He helped millions of people to the dismay of the medical profession. He died with no money, from over doing himself to help others. He only died in January of 1945. His son supplies books from his fathers' notes that tell of the cures he gave out. Patrick Berkery Ph.D. wrote about him and his cures. He used peanut oil rub downs for Arthritis.

This mans story started groups of college students and teachers in the practice of leaving their bodies with their souls and traveling else where, then returning to their bodies again. A close friend in college in 1962, told me of several instances when he had left his body. Sometimes travel was frightening. Other times he would travel anywhere. Another person I worked with told me one time he was very sick and left his body for a few moments. His senses and sight rose up. He could see his body lying in the motel room, then returned. He could hardly tell who the body was. It seemed so swelled up and out of its normal shape. The doctors later said he nearly died that night. Doctors said he had a reaction to penicillin given him during the day, for his illness. He and I both know he came close to dying that night. His soul did leave his body, but then returned because it was not yet his time to die.

This is what the dying woman on the road experienced. She was with her Dad's soul gone from his dead body just before the daughter 1000 miles away.

People, who have tried to commit suicide interviewed on a TV show said, when they left their bodies they saw bad images. Apprehensive they went back into their bodies. They would never try suicide again. Others who have left their bodies felt such a calm they almost did not come back to life again. Cayce on the other hand felt tired if he left his body too many times. He also felt he could will himself any where he wanted. With the written record and the books you can buy, he sure did what he said he could.

A husband and wife team Semyon and Valentine Kirlian both medical doctors in Russia took pictures of peoples spirit or aura's. A person missing an arm physically, had the out line of the arm show in the picture. The Kirlians did this with plants too. Cut off leaves, took a picture of the plant and the outline of the leaf was still there. They did this by using radio waves on the people and plants while taking the picture. It activated the electrical field we have been calling spirit or aura's or Entity. Activated the entity would show up on film. Some of this information shown on television once or twice, then became old news.

I read a book called "THE HUMAN BIOMAGNETIC AURA" from a college library. A buddy of mine who had gone to college knew about it. When he read one of my original papers he gave me the book. Another friend gave me a book "THE ELECTRO DYNAMIC THEORY OF LIFE." The books author a law professor at Yale university, Doctor Northrop. After these two books it begins to make me wonder about people of the mental ability's gift of genius. Who gets these gifts? More study brought to light the fact that most of the genius in the world came from Europe. So what is so different about Europe? Then I found it in one of my books on navigation.

The Flux of the Van Allen belts that encircle the earth move. The swinging movement changes the magnetic compass. Navigators must allow mathematically for this over long distances. More movement is on record in Europe than anywhere else. If we would build a machine that would vary a magnetic flux around our heads we might become very smart people. I have worked on this for a number of years, but can show no evidence. Someone will come up with it by 2000.

I am sure I must be doing something wrong. Look at **FIGURE 8**. These are the Van Allen Belts around our earth. They were only proven in January of 1958 by explorer one. They very closely resemble an electric motor flux field. The Van Allen belts would be the field and the earth rotating would be the Armature. The Sun supplies the current for the field of this motor or the Van Allen belts. The earth speeds up and slows down in relationship to the strength of the Sun's Current and changes in our Van Allen belts. The speed changes every year, proportional to the 3,000,000 mile difference from the sun in December and June.

Early in the 1940's, in Ohio, I remember as a young boy on my bicycle the great beams of light in the night sky. All colors. They resembled search lights pointed toward the top of the sky. Everyone said it was the Northern lights. Northern Lights are electric flux rays from the Sun hitting the Van Allen belts and causing the color streamers in the sky. Could that have been a sign as is spoken of in the Bible? We had World War 2 happen in December of 1941 didn't

Motors exchange currents in
their flux fields between the
Armature and coils. This
causes the Armature of
the motor to turn.

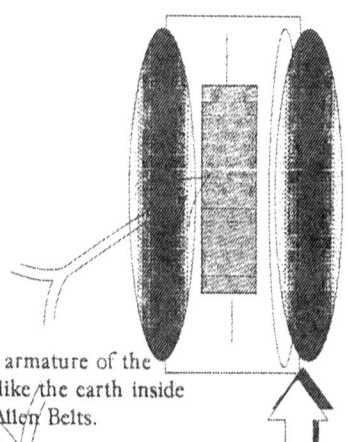

Magnetic armature of the
motor is like the earth inside
the Van Allen Belts.

The flux fields of the motor turn
the magnetic armature.

The field of the Earth or the
Van Allen Belts receive their
current from the Sun's rays and
the Earth turns like the Armature
in the motor. The speed of the
Earth Changes each year with
the distance of the Sun from
the Earth.

# FIGURE 8

43

## Magnetic Birthday Chart

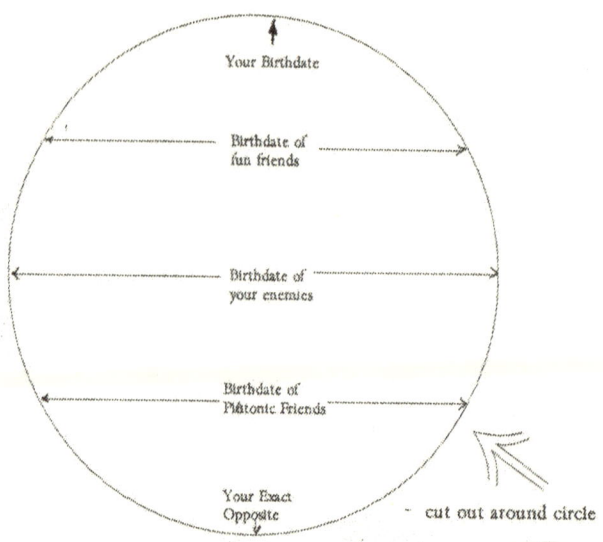

Your Birthdate

Birthdate of
fun friends

Birthdate of
your enemies

Birthdate of
Platonic Friends

Your Exact
Opposite

cut out around circle

# Figure 10

we? This thinking is what developed the Mood Wheel you used earlier in this book.

Here is another wheel like figure 2. It measures the strength of relationships between people the same way you would measure a magnetic coil. See **FIGURE 10** disk. Cut it out and fit it over the large disk figure 3 like the last chart we made. Turn the pointer at the top to November 25 again. Now you can read direct the magnetic reaction to each of the other birth dates involved. There is a happy flux with the FUN FRIENDS who have birthdays on 25 September on the right side, and 25 January on the left side. The enemy's birthdays are 25 August on the right side of the wheel and 25 February on the left side of the wheel. The close platonic friend for life on the left side is 25 March and on the right is 25 July. Finally you can find the exact opposite listed below as 25 May. This will work for anyone using it the same way as the example birthday. You have about two dates on either side of the exact dates listed that will have the same reactions.

There is another wheel that will work for you, so maybe the book has been worth the moneys after all. Please realize that there are many variables in your chart. These can weaken or strengthen your friends and enemies listed on this wheel. You will find the listed birth dates on our chart to be very accurate. Check out the friends you already have. They of course are the relationship to your sun sign and other's sun signs. Did I hear the word Astrology? With my mention of it, let's take a look at it.

I hate the word Astrology because of the association with Witches, voodoo and the like. Let's go back to our Bible for just a minute. Remember when UI or God made the firmament in GENESIS CHAPTER 1 VERSE 14. He indicated these lights were for signs and seasons.

He also did this just prior to setting up Adam and Eve on earth. What if, Just what if this firmament and the lights in it were a BLUEPRINT for the plans of UI or God? It makes sense that anyone building anything of any size would have a blueprint now wouldn't it? Just his handiwork it said in PSALMS 19:1 & 2. What do you know! In PSALMS 8:3-6 it says he ordained these stars and moon. Well dog gone look at Hebrews 9:23-24. Christ himself purified the stars and moon. Why was purification so important for the stars and the moon? BECAUSE DEAR FRIENDS, LIKE IT OR NOT, THE FIRMAMENT CARRIES GOD'S BLUEPRINT, AND ITS NOT TO BE CHANGED BY ANYONE. Josephus a noted Jewish historian says in his book 2, Chapter 7, and Verse 2 that Abraham was very skillful in the celestial sciences. Oh my, never heard that before! Think I am off the wall with this? READ IT FOR YOURSELF. Don't bother to ask your preacher cause he dose not want to hear about it. There is no money in this kind of Preaching. Give money for you sin's and be saved.

Look up the word (SIGNS) in any Bible concordance. Read all of the references to the word (SIGNS) in the Bible. The book of Revelations shows that during tribulations the stars and moon are dark. WHY? Well, because GOD removes the gift of his blueprint so you don't know what is coming. Did you know that the three Wise men who found CHRIST were star gazers? The original word for wise men is MAGIAN. This means Persian astronomers or priest's. Yes, it's in the Bible concordances. Why else would people be outside watching the sky and following stars that moved in the sky? If their job was to watch the sheep, how did they see the star move? Also note that today's Astronomers came from Astrologers down in history, and that priest's and the leaders of the day in past history were Astrologers.

I know, you went to your preacher and he said "Read Jeremiah 10:2," Okay! Let's just do that right now. Everyone read it. PREACHERS ALSO READ IT AGAIN. Jeremiah 10:2 "Learn not the way of the heathen and be not dismayed, at the signs of Heaven; for the heathen are dismayed at them." What is the meaning of DISMAYED? "To fill with apprehension, petrify with uneasiness. To make greatly troubled, to depress." Since I am **NOT** a heathen, (a non Christian) I don't have to worry do I? Preachers have used this one passage for years and years. It's the only verse they have and they mislead you with what it means, or perhaps they are mislead by what it means. **IF YOU'RE NOT A HEATHEN**, THEN **DON'T** BE DISMAYED AT THE SIGNS OF HEAVEN. Simple isn't it?

Let's look at the Lords sample prayer in Matthew 6:9. "Our Father which art in heaven, hallowed be thy name." "Thy kingdom come, Thy will be done in earth, as it is in heaven." Stop right there. What does that mean "done in earth as it is in heaven"? It means as the signs and seasons of heaven say, it will be done on earth. Yes, what Gods blueprint says, will be done on earth, every single hour of the day, and day of the week. You will repeat the lessons you need to become compatible with a life of perfection with GOD. Only then can we accept GOD AND HIS PERFECTION'S. Until then, we will keep on doing, on earth as it is in the heaven, and until we get it right…..

Well, have you left me yet? If you're looking at this book again and are ready to sneak in another paragraph or so, let's do it together. God made a blueprint guide for us to use in our lives down here on earth, so that school would not get too hard for us. He wants us to win. He wants us to pass the test's. Every single test, so he put the answers to the tests in heaven in this blueprint.

If I am the only one, stupid enough to believe this, why is it that Chinese records show Emperor Yao divided the twelve signs of the zodiac, 2300 years BC? An Egyptian named Imhotep did horoscopes in 2667 BC. Imhotep was the architect of the pyramid at Saqqarah. Mayan records from the 800 to 1500 centuries were 70 percent perfect cause they used astrology. Copernicus believed and used Astrology and he was so smart he figured out that the planets rotate around the sun. Babylonian astrologers were the ruling class of the Chaldeans. Ptolemy of Egypt used and believed in astrology. Tycho Brahe an astronomer used and wrote horoscopes for the king's family in 1577. Johannes Keplers choose his wife from her astrological chart. The inventor of logarithms John Hapier and Scottish genius of math used and believed Astrology. He devised the logarithms to speed up his Astrology work. India used astrology to make compatible marriages, and it proved to have worked well. The twelve sons of Jacob and Ishmael in Genesis Chapter's 25-48-49 compare each son with the twelve Houses of astrology. The twelve gates of Jerusalem described by Ezekiel were zodiacal in their locations and descriptions. Shakespeare's work references astrology, all the time. Ben Franklin's Almanac showed astrology as a way of life, along with his weather predictions and planting information. President F. D. Roosevelt openly used Astrologers advice. Adolph Hitler openly used 5 astrologer's advice and only lost the war because he stopped using their advice. Even Nancy Reagan got caught using astrologers to help her husband the president, so she must damn well believe in the studies. J. F. Kennedy University at Martinez California has a fully accredited course on astrology.

How much does it take friends to show you the truth? Did anyone ever mention about the massive computer that is in Chicago Illinois? It's shaped much like an upside down cross, and jokingly it's called 666 by University of Illinois students. The first, middle, or last name, a street number, street name, social security number, telephone number, license number (any type of license) will give pages of information on every dollar you ever had, or spent or borrowed. Even your neighbor's names, your friend's information, your houses, cars, schooling, almost every thing you own. Every birth record is in it. A computer like this is an awful thing for anyone to have and use, and worst yet, to laugh about.

Well, every one has been using astrology information on us for years. Every time you fill out anything you must put down your date of birth, DAY, MONTH, YEAR. Yes, it is true, you can't know every detail of a person without the exact time, and place of birth, but the information on just the day month and year will tell you a lot.

A book written in 1930 by Grant Lewi entitled "HEAVEN KNOWS WHAT" is one of the few book's I ever suggest to anyone besides the Bible. Lewi's book will give you loads of information about people with just their DAY, MONTH, AND YEAR. Grant Lewi was a teacher at a well-known college when directed into astrology by his future mother in law. He set out to prove the study stupid and wrong as many people have, and become hooked on the truth about astrology.

Grant Lewi wrote a second book before he died in 1951. "ASTROLOGY FOR THE MILLIONS." This book requires the time of birth also, but will tell you when your success will be, when you will fail, when you will be popular and when you will be unpopular in life. An interesting fact about Grant Lewi was he never believed in insurance until 1950 when he purchased a life policy, just one year before his death. This indicates he had found the key in Astrology, that tells you when the chances are of your dying.

Evangeline Adams wrote a book "ASTROLOGY, YOUR PLACE AMONG THE STARS" in 1930 that tells you when you will be sick and from what, but you should be into astrology for a few years before you read that one.

Astrology will tell you anything you wish to know. When you will be sick or well, when you will be successful and when you will fail and why, when you will marry and will it last or not, who is right for you to marry and why, how your children will turn out.

There is just nothing you can't know from astrology, but like anything else, there are good astrologers and poor astrologers. Buying book after book is an error. I spent thousands of dollars just finding about 10 books that told the truth and are useful. Most books on astrology will lead you from book to book just to make money from you, so don't buy anything except what I have listed, unless you have lots of time and money that is.

Now I have the publishers mad at me too, but I don't like publishers much either. I have a few people who like me. Well, LET THOSE WHO HAVE EARS HEAR, AND THOSE WHO HAVE EYES SEE. The rest can just continue being dumb and used by others.

Have you made it this far? Okay, let's review again! Before Adam and Eve there was a perfect earth with perfect people. One of them got greedy and talked one third of the people to follow him like sheep. Everyone lost their bodies and had only (electric Entities) or souls. The one third hated being without bodies! The other two thirds received a reward by jobs to do for God. God then refurbished the earth, made a blueprint of what he proposed to do and put Adam and Eve on the planet to start our schooling.

We live, learn, die, return to learn more, die, return to learn more, and when we have learned enough to know how to handle the gift of paradise, that God has for us, we don't have to return anymore. The ones who give up in their schooling by committing suicide go with the one third lost souls without any bodies.

Check out this theory. Read Revelations 3:12. It says, "HE SHALL GO NO MORE OUT." Read! Don't take any body's word for it. What other possible meaning could it have? Thomas Edison believed in reincarnation openly.

Okay let's explore some other things. Weather on our planet is nothing more than positive and negative masses of charged particles. These cells move around due to winds (which are positive or negative also). When there is a mass of water collected by these weather cells (clouds) the water squeezes out like a sponge by temperature changes.

A man known as **Doctor Nikola Tesla** discovered how to bounce weather cells off an alternating radio wave and thereby redirect weather cells. President Jimmy Carter during his presidency signed a treaty with USSR that neither country would use this system to redirect weather. This all means that positives and negatives can control weather cells.

People are positive sometimes, and sometimes negative. What if a huge mass of people all put out the same magnetic signal either positive or negative at the same time and attracted weather systems? Then you could say that mass thinking directed a weather cell to them, and might have caused flooding, or in some case's drought. It is not impossible you know, just hard to prove. What if the one third of the electrical entities working for lucifer directed the weather cells? If we the people could help, would they do it on their own? NO! WE MUST ASK FOR THEIR HELP BY PRAYER, just as the Bible says.

Doctor Tesla is another good example of a cover up. He is the man who presented alternating voltage to the world. We all know Edison made the light bulb! We are lead to believe he made our electrical systems. In truth Edison believed in direct power like batteries. This is what he would have used in our world. Direct power would only travel up in buildings about two

51

floors high! We would have had a large power plant every 30 square mile on the earth to get power to everyone. Dr. Tesla is the man who, invented radio, invented alternating power, invented the dynamotors to generate alternating power, and is responsible for the light and alternating power all over the world today. TOP COLLEGE STUDENTS ON THE JEOPARDY TV SHOW HAD NEVER HEARD OF HIS NAME. LORD, WHAT A SHAME……..

When he died in 1943 the United States GOVERNMENT grabbed everything he had on paper and all of his equipment and hid it somewhere. When Yugoslavia complained (country where he was born) the USA sent some token papers and equipment, but kept hidden the large part of his works. Nowhere in the history books do they mention Doctor Tesia. Not one time in our schools' systems is his name! The world owes our lights and power systems to his genius alone. Therefore school history is in error as it stands.

The famous Wright brothers were the first to power flight in history! **NO!** We never heard of the powered airplane in France nine months **BEFORE** the Wright ever left the ground!

Only five months after the famous **Rosewell** incident of a UFO crash in 1947, the Transistor came into being. Up till then vacuum tubes were the top of the line. The industry had just graduated into the Peanut size vacuum tube! THEN CAME THE TRANSISTOR OUT OF NOWHERE. Three men at Bell labs developed it over night. Bill Shockley, John Bardeen and Walt Brattain. It then took till 1971 for the microprocessor chip to be developed and micro electronics to really take hold. They studied that UFO equipment and got their ideas from it.

What about the book "THE GREAT POWER LINE COVER UP" by Paul Brodeur, when the USA keeps telling us it's all okay? It's like the money spending cover up in Washington DC.

The lying started at your birth and will continued till your death. The ability of Astrology a true science is also part of that lie. It's so bad that states won't allow the time of birth applied to certificates any more. I think the time has come when the world should wake up. You can't believe what they told you in school. To find the truth you look for it on your own. Most people find it much easier to sit and listen and believe rather than read for the truth. Ross Perot uses this fact over and over. So will every preacher. It is easier to sit and listen and believe, rather than read for the truth.

I hope with this small little book to alert at least some of you who will read! The facts I am sharing with you are at least a beginning.

Astrology dumped in the 1700-1800 period became Astronomy, the science of the stars. Religions proclaimed that Astrology was a superstition and so it remains. World War 2 saw the destruction of records and libraries of astrologic information. Of course the Catholic Church has the bulk of the information on astrology stored secretly for its own use. I just can't help feel, now is the time for the world to find out some of these facts. I am giving you the chance to grow in your knowledge and gain from it.

The sky you see in your part of the world, moves all of the time, and started when God refurbished the earth. It moves very little itself. The earth spinning makes it move in our eyes about 30 degrees each 4 minutes.

The ever changing blueprint in the firmament is the key to our evolution on earth each minute of the day. Arguments against Astrology have used the erratic movement of the planet earth to discredit the science. The fact is the erratic movement's of the earth's poles are what draw the map we read. At the first breath you take after birth the map overhead is your blue print.

Even twins born over 4 minutes apart are different and it shows in their blueprint. I know your thinking "WELL WHAT ABOUT THE OTHER THOUSANDS OF BABY'S TAKING NEW BREATH AROUND THE WORLD?" That's a fair question. If you would put a map of your state on the ceiling of your room, and you stood in the center and looked up you would see a view of your state. If you move to the lower right corner of the room when you looked up at the ceiling you would have a completely different view of your state. Then moving to the upper left corner of the room you would again have a completely different view of your state.

Your birth locations decide what your map looks like. The Day, Month, Year, Time, and location account for the **ONLY EXACT** map of your birth. Once you freeze this map on a piece of paper an astrologer can determine many things. You're moods by the day of each month; You're mental abilities and capacities; You're sexual outlook in life; You're perfect mate with their birth date; You're health prospects over your life; You're time of success and failure in life; You're mental out look positive and negative over your life; You're periods of possible separation or divorce, and your change of life periods with the details.

Now with just the DAY, MONTH, AND YEAR you can get a reasonable description of yourself in life. Without that time and place, it's lacking in all of the details. Remember I smile 4 minutes can make a difference? Think about the Doctor who thinks you were born about 6 PM or 4 PM with no idea that the first breath is so important, and how far off was the clock he used in his guess? The time changes one hour ahead in some places and one hour back in other places! How much better our lives would be with a little less interference and more exact details. Money is more valuable than gifts that cost nothing but time to read about them. Let those who have ears, hear.

With this frozen map a good Astrologer can tell you what to expect from your children and when. It can tell you when to conceive and birth your children so they fit into your family and give you tons of love instead of being a total burden. They can even tell you when you will have females or males at birth and how to decide this factor in your life. If you have a computer of any size at all, you can buy a program that will draw out any map for DAY, MONTH, YEAR, TIME, AND PLACE. It's as good as I can do using paper, pencil, logarithm's and several hours of work in about 3 minutes. Call John Halloran 1-800-732-4628. His programs are the best I have ever seen.

The reading of the map will vary with who does the reading quite a little bit. Even the computer will give it a try. Details in your life will be reasonably close.

This map is a picture of the sky at the time of your first breath that becomes divided into 12 signs, with 9 planets. The 12 signs have three sectors each. The planets have different levels of power due to their locations in the map. Each planet can use its value for or against other planets. Some will stand out more, others almost concealed. Using all of this is how an Astrologer can give you the percentages of chance for things happening in your life. You were born with a **FREE WILL** to do what you want. This free will is in this chart or map. The chart or map shows the lessons you will have to experience during your life time. How you react to these experiences is still up to you.

The map's value is to let you know ahead about the road you must travel, therefore you can make judgments that will ease the experiences or for that matter make the experiences even harder.

On Television you see all the talk show hosts trying to guide people down the road of life. TV preachers giving you advise and know nothing about you.

All of his advice, all of this money, and direction are as near as your birth certificate, for free. We can't all be Astrologers can we, so let's say for $40 or $50 dollars we could buy a chart that would be like a road map to our lives. Pity is that most of you would not take heed of anything an Astrologer could give you, because you have your minds made up it is all just so much hokis-pokis. If your life looked good, then you would believe it, but if it's something you don't want to hear, then trash that thing. Don't study it and find an easier way. You might have to exert some patience. Nobody has that today do we? No time, no patience, no value for lives, no value for justice, no time to vote out the crooks in our Government. This world is a mess isn't it? Well, we made it that way, each and every one of us have played a part in what is going on around us. The easy way is the only way and the easy way is to let the other guy do it. I am too busy trying to out-buy my neighbor in material things. He gets a new car so, I must have one too. He gets a girl friend, I must have one. He makes a fortune with drugs. Then I must get in on the money too. He gets killed early in life with little to show for the pain! You only live once, live it to the hilt.

W R O N G! We will have to come back and when we do we will have to pay back the bad stuff we dealt out in that other life. It's called the law of KARMA or the law of cause and effect. You will pay back for your mistakes. The AKASHIC books of soul records never fail to be right.

Edgar Cayce the healer said he had seen these records during one of his out of the body experiences while going to read another soul that needed healing. Edgar Cayce was a truly gifted man. The burdens must have been a very heavy load to carry trying to heal all that ask, and he did it for no payment. How proud God must have been to have someone like Edgar Cayce to help him. How awful God must feel when one of our TV preachers rips off poor folks in the name of Jesus, his only son.

You ever notice that a church won't even recognize a preacher unless he comes from their teaching school? Can't have anyone preach something we don't want our people to hear.

While I was in the Church of Christ near Columbus Ohio the local preacher gave us lessons on Revelations for about a month telling us about the coming of Christ. Then he went on vacation while a traveling Church of Christ preacher and his family in their bus came in for a big revival. This guy was good. He could really preach until one night he took off on Revelations. His preaching was with verse after verse of proof that Christ had already come and we were close to the end. The traveling preacher had picked up on the Ah—millennial Theory of Revelations. Our local preacher had preached on the Post-millennial theory of revelations. This says Jesus will return again soon. Both preachers were good until they came together on the last night and confronted the theories of Revelations. Two thirds of the congregation left the church over this little show of theories. The traveling preacher out preached the local. All the local preacher said was, "It will be okay, I can build a new congregation in about four months."

The plight of the people did not mean one thing to either preacher. Sound like organized religion? I left that church and went in and out of 4 different churches looking for the truth. Finally in the last Baptist Bible preaching church I found a home. Of course that lasted only a year till the fact came out that the preacher was having sex with six females in the singing group. That was the last time I went to learn from another man. I turned to God and ask for help and the truth. I received it with the science of Astrology. I find so few to share my findings with. I have a faith in God that has opened up a new out look on life for me. Everything I see has the holy spirit in it and I value each and every little thing for the real value of it's teaching and loving power.

Consider the people we have seen that have been sick all of their lives. Seemed so unfair didn't it? Maybe, they were receiving back something they had done to someone else in a past life. Would it seem so unfair under those conditions?

How about the poor who are starving and cold. This would seem so unfair right? Well, if this was what they had done to another in some past life, it would change the whole picture would it not? So you see, with Karma involved in our lives, life turns out to be, lesson after lesson, and God is not such a bad guy as some people think. He is just the father type who is trying to teach his family right from wrong with "ON THE JOB TRAINING." We also must remember that our souls agreed to these lessons prior to them happening, because our soul knew down deep that we needed these experiences in order to grow into that final perfect soul, God desires us to be.

Did you know that today "October 31, 1993" it's snowing in Ohio? Cincinnati yesterday received five and one half inches unexpectedly, and set new records in the books.

As I sit here typing I can't help thinking with the spread of knowledge, our world would in advance know the weather. We would be able to help areas in advance of floods, fires, etc. Ben Franklin started the almanac for just that purpose. It would require astrology people in many areas caring for each area in order to do it properly. The USA is so big it's hard to chart the entire country and be correct in all areas. If we all shared our knowledge many people could take up the task, but of course if it won't make any money, who wants to do it. A very few have the desire just to know the truth. We buy books, read them, but never follow up with effort to change that which we can change. We always let someone else do it. This outlook should stop. It would change the entire world. Remember MONEY IS THE ROUTE OF ALL EVIL, and it shows in almost everything we do.

We know for instance that on 8 November 1993 around 8:00 A.M. Venus and Jupiter will show history no one should miss. However few will find it of any interest. History will go by and it didn't seem news worthy to the big TV stations. A few preachers will call it a vision or miracle and another FATIMA will be born, Oh no! I have lost the rest of the Catholics now.

It's hard for any Astrologer to think people find no interest in the future. The USA natal (frozen) chart, with planets moving in it, (transit's) have indicated our conditions since the early 1900's. I will show you a short example from 1971 on.

1971-1984 Upheaval in human relationships (planet 1 indicates).
Emotional problems, search of long life (planet 2 indicates).

1981-1989 Challenge to religion's and preachers (planet 2 indicates.

1988-1996 Crisis in all traditional & established structures (planet 2 indicates).

1984-1995 A giant sexual Revolution with investigation & experience (planet 1).

1995-2008 New space travel, religious intensity (planet 1).

1995-2003 New communications, revolutionary ideas.

In 1971 and 1972 I told a group of my students and friends that by 1993 the (HAVE NOT'S) would be revolting against the (HAVE'S). They would be taking by force what they wanted. I am almost sure that the Kennedy Brothers knew this also. They pushed so hard for gun control when at the White House. Only those who had ears would hear, and there were just not enough who listened. Even today as it is happening and people are expiring in the streets, no one will listen.

We find money for the exploration of the Moon and outer space, which has to date, done very little for us, so the government has put a slow down to further money for further projects. We could spend money for projects much more suitable to improving our life here on this planet, but as you can figure out, it's just not the right time yet.

Congress will not give up there under the table incomes from space contractors, so they fight to continue the spending to go back to the moon, and go to mars. We need only take care of earth, nothing else.

My daughter who lives in California tells me I could make a fortune in Astrology out west. In the East few find it worth their interest. People who are happy never want to investigate. The unhappy people are the ones who search me out and ask, "WHEN AM I GOING TO GET OVER THIS PERIOD IN MY LIFE?" Always, when I show them their past and the future, they leave pleased that they know the answer to all of their questions. Few ever redirect their lives for the betterment of their future. It is for the betterment of their dollar income, in most cases.

If life is difficult, people want advice and desire to know the future. I told one lady about her daughter who was going from an optimistic popular A student, to a pessimistic unpopular failure in her later years in high school. Her reaction was one of "This just can't be. She is the best daughter in the world. Your science is just not correct." I didn't hear from her again until the daughter had left school and ran away. She could have put the girl in a school with more discipline and avoided the present problem. The girl's education would allow her to become a well-educated adult. Instead, she is just another drug addict.

How about the airline pilot with his 4 poor hours during a landing or take off with 200 passengers on board? How many lives would his mood charts save?

Ever notice someone start a business and it just goes down the tubes. At another time in the same building and the same business, another person succeeds. The business had a day, month, year, time, and place of birth, just like people. A good astrologer could have helped the first business in its starting date and saved a lot of money. Remember Ecclesiastes 3:1-8; "TO EVERY THING THERE IS A SEASON, AND A TIME TO EVERY PURPOSE UNDER THE HEAVEN."

Every purpose under the heaven means just that. When you conceive your child, you determine the approximate birth period. You can mold the child to fit into your family. The birth times of your vacation determine you're having a good time or not. If you choose the right person to marry, and the best time to marry, it can make all the difference in the world in the length and outcome of your marriage. When you're in love, who will listen?

I had a step son who would not listen. He wanted lots of kids and I told him the girl he was to marry did not want kids. After marriage, we seldom saw him. His in-laws understood him far better than we. They had a baby, a new house, new truck, new car. All purchased at the wrong time and for the wrong reasons. They divorced when my step son found no more children. His wife, had her tubes tied after the first child. They lost the house. The truck rusted to the ground in only a few years.

He almost lost the car. He ignores the ex-in-laws and hates me because I had forewarned him of all of these things happening. He acts as if I made them happen. When you can't help your kids, whom can you help? LET THOSE WHO HAVE EARS, HEAR!

If you buy your house at the right time it can be a pleasure always. If your home is all problems, chances are you choose the wrong time to buy, maybe even the wrong area.

Ever had a car that was a lemon? Many people have, yet we neglect to notice how many of the same cars are on the road for 130,000 miles with no trouble hardly at all. It was the wrong time to buy for this person.

Would you believe that one planet can indicate a disturbance in all types of communications? Radio, telephones, even messages become misunderstood. Orders that are totally wrong when you get them. Ever notice that all of our appliances break down at once? If one breaks down, another will follow. One planet can indicate this in our astrology maps. PLEASE NOTICE, I said INDICATE! NOT MAKE HAPPEN! The sky is a map and I don't feel or know of any force that can cause these things to happen. I do know however that maps and planets can sure INDICATE these things are going to happen.

When JFK's assassination took place, every single Astrologer knew it would happen. Jean Dixon got all of the publicity and credit because she has the money to promote and advertise herself, but it was no surprise to those who watched the planets.

What about the people who go to get a ticket for a plane trip and decide to go later due to INTUITION. Later they find the plane they decided not to take crashed, and killed everyone. It is not luck. It was not their time to die and that INTUITION was the spirit working for them.

"TO EVERY THING THERE IS A SEASON AND A TIME TO EVERY PURPOSE UNDER THE HEAVEN."

"LET THOSE WHO HAVE EARS HEAR"

Remember EVANGELINE ADAMS I talked about earlier? This was the author who can tell you when you will be sick and from what. Her husband one time had a bad accident that injured his face. First thing she did was look on her charts to see if his accident was major or minor. The map showed it a minor accident. She informed her husband he would not lose his eye. Of course he did not lose the eye, and the accident was minor, although at the time it looked very major.

The Solar System within the Milky Way is a picture of a human body cell within our bodies. Every thing has a nucleus with a sphere or numerous spheres around it. I read a book one time that said consider that our bodies made up of many cells, reflect millions of Solar Systems. Humorous? How big is the universe? The world still can't believe the earth is like a motor. People who know electronics believe the truth.

Ever hear of the LAW OF COMPOUND PROBABILITY? It refers to the chances of a prediction being true.

As an example: "A PREDICTION WITH TWO DETAILS HAS ONE CHANGE IN FOUR OF COMING TO PASS."

This explains why Jean Dixon seldom is correct in her predictions since the JFK shooting! Read her predictions each year. How many are right, One in one hundred? She's all money and not too good at Astrology I'm afraid.

Here is a brief chart of the Law of Compound Probability.

| Number of Detail | Fulfillment is one chance in |
|---|---|
| 1 | 2 |
| 2 | 4 |
| 3 | 8 |
| 4 | 16 |
| 5 | 32 |
| 6 | 64 |
| 7 | 128 |
| 8 | 256 |

This means the mood chart that you have by now found to work very well, (within a few hours give or take) has 8 predictions of details. Therefore the chance of fulfillment is one in 256. It will work, and each time with no fails. Just adjust to your birth time. Astrology will work all of the time too, if done right, with all details including time and place.

You must allow a little error for the time considering that all of our watches are not exact, and all Doctors are not precise about the time, and all areas are not under the same time zone regulations. Indiana for example is the hardest state to calculate. Each municipality change's time as they please. It is hard to keep tract of all the changes in the US. There is a thick book that covers all of the USA. It gives the history of time in each state according to municipal records. It helps, but still does not have all of the answers. It's hard to stay ahead of all of the Governments changes in each state.

The book "CELESTIAL INFLUENCE" by Rodney Collin gives information about cycles in our universe that you will find hard to believe. These cycles are true because they have repeated themselves for years and records are on file. Rodney's book will also show you how transformers work and how we are all electrical in our make up. Smart man. LET THOSE HOW HAVE EARS HEAR.

Have you lived long enough to notice some of the old movie stars starting to emerge again? At my age you will notice it. When they were very popular they were IN THE FISH BOWL. Every one noticed them. Then they just went away. You stopped hearing of them. Then in about a little over 23 years, here they come popping up on TV AND RADIO shows again.

Fashions are the same way. I hear that the fashions of 1993 are almost a duplicate of the 1970's. Guess that is about 23 years isn't it? Of course I know nothing about fashions and never will.

Remember hearing "HISTORY WILL REPEAT ITSELF"? When you have lived long enough you will see that it does repeat itself. That is if you take the time to notice. Most people never have the time to notice anything, except how much the pay check is and if it is on time or not.

The above is leading up to the fact that the Planet Saturn cycles a complete orbit in about 29 years, which is why history repeats itself in 23 to 29 year periods.

Other cycles are:

| | |
|---|---|
| Cotton prices every | 8 years |
| Stock market & suicides | 9 years |
| Salmon catch | 9.6 years |
| U.S. Weather, sunspots | 11.2 years |
| Wars | 15 years |
| Real Estate, building | 18 years |
| Church membership | 9 years |
| Marriage rates | 18.2 years |
| U. S. IMMIGRATION | 18.2 years |
| Airplane traffic | 5.2 years |
| General Electric Orders | 6 years |
| Aluminum Production | 6.4 years |

Life Insurance Sales                9 years
U. S. WET AND DRY CYCLES            25 years

Murder in U.S. is up every June July August. Auto Theft in the U.S. peaks in December to February.

There is a FOUNDATION FOR THE STUDY OF CYCLES. They have a book called "CYCLES" The mysterious Forces that Trigger Events, printed in 1971 it gives much information.

The "CYCLES OF BECOMING," (Planetary Pattern of Growth) by Alexander Ruperti really opens up the cycles involving a person's life, but without ears to hear you won't understand it.

Edmond Halley was a famous astronomer who admired Sir Isaac Newton's Principia Mathematica (the theory of universal gravitation). Halley used it to calculate the return years of a comet discovered by Dorffel on the August 15, 1682. You have heard of Halley's Comet? It seems that Newton and Halley went around and around about Astrology one time. Halley told Newton he did not believe in Astrology. Newton simply said he had studied the subject and that Halley had not. LET THOSE WHO HAVE EARS HEAR.

Lets look at some facts you can find in your Natal (frozen at birth) chart. Look at FIGURE 11. This is a map of the heavens frozen in place with DAY, MONTH, YEAR, TIME, AND PLACE OF BIRTH. We call this a (NATAL MAP). We are going to look at transit planets (those that keep moving beyond the frozen birth map).

NOTE: PLANETS MOVE ALL OF THE TIME. IN A BIRTH MAP WE FREEZE THE MAP (NATAL MAP), SO WE CAN SEE THE BLUEPRINT AT THAT VERY MOMENT.

THE PLANETS KEEP RIGHT ON MOVING AND IF WE WATCH THEM MOVE OVER THE FROZEN (NATAL) MAP, WE CALL THE MOVEMENT OF THE PLANETS TRANSIT'S.

We will view the moving planets as they progress on the frozen map. I have not put any frozen planet locations or the signs in the (NATAL) map to keep it sample. In **FIGURE 11** you will find an A on the left side of the circle in house number 1, and B at the bottom in house number 3, a C on the right side in house number 7, with a D at the top in house number 10. Locate these in FIGURE 11.

Lets use Jupiter as our first example. Jupiter is a planet that INDICATES health, mental outlook and popularity. Like all planets it moves around the map in an anti-clockwise direction or opposite of your clock at home. It moves about one time around this map each 12 years. Each person has Jupiter at a different place in the Natal (frozen birth) map according to their time of birth, so these INDICATIONS of Jupiter I will describe, will happen at different years, for different people.

When Jupiter transit's (or moves from year to year) from A house number 1 through B house number 3, your mental outlook is very pessimistic or depressed. With a negative outlook, you are subject to illness of many kinds. Your body is un-informed to fight off sickness by your mind. Ever hear of the POWER OF POSITIVE THINKING? Well, A through B is the power of negative thinking. Norman Vincent Peal was a famous man of religion in the early 1900's who wrote books on this power of positive thinking. Some people have a strong location of Jupiter in the frozen

# FROM A TO D TO C IS CONSIDERED THE "FISH BOWL AREA".

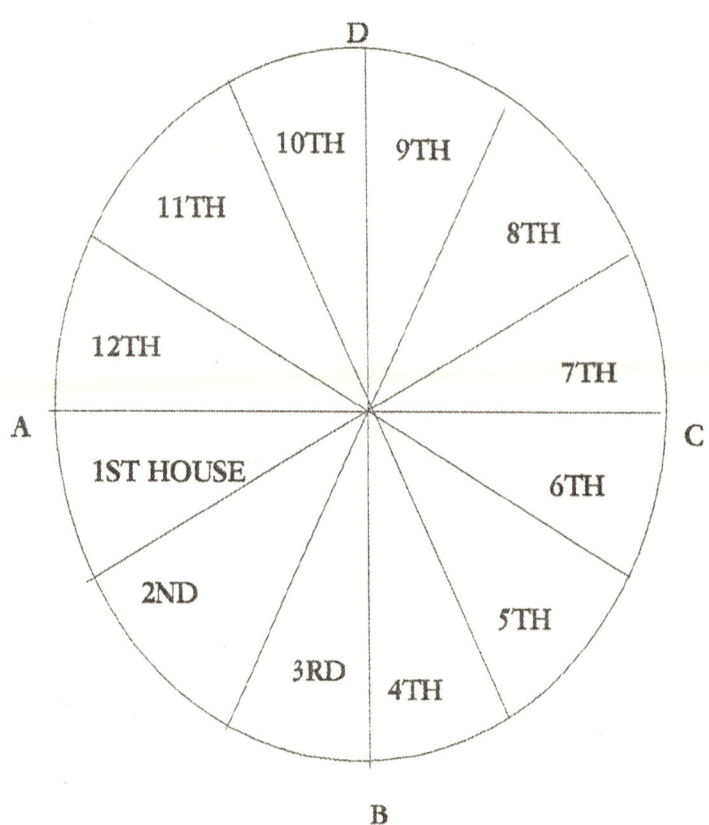

THIS CHART IS THE SKY DIRECTLY ABOVE YOU AT YOUR BIRTH AND IS DIVIDED INTO THE 12 HOUSES OR SECTIONS IN ORDER TO REFINE ANY READINGS BY ASTROLOGERS. PLANETS ARE PLACED HERE ALSO AND READ.

## FIGURE 11

(NATAL) maps at the time of birth, and are positive most of their lives. Vincent Peal must have been one of those people. A person with a weak location of Jupiter in the frozen (NATAL) maps at birth, become negative much of their life. The positive people can't understand why others are negative. Negative people wonder how positive people can be positive all of the time.

This A to B area makes you very unpopular also. You find yourself with very few friends. It is a perfect time for studies and learning while your mind is in neutral. Your brain is working well and lacks concern for life outside.

As Jupiter's transit's (or moves from year to year) from B to C you find that your heavy depression leaves. You are sick less and less, and on occasion you have a positive thought.

As Jupiter transit's (or moves from year to year) into C area, you find people smile at you. You begin to gather friends again. Jupiter transit's to the D level you will be very popular. Your never sick or depressed and if you should have a major illness (indicated by some other planet that is transiting in the natal map), you will recover very quickly with Jupiter here. This lasts till Jupiter moves back into the A position again. We call from C to D to A the FISH BOWL AREA, because everyone notices your presents. After Jupiter transit's below A, you're right back where you were when we started. Read A to B again.

Now this is only one planet as it transit's around your Natal map. WE have eight other planets we know about The Bible says in Genesis 37: 9, "The Sun and the Moon and the Eleven Stars." So, we could have 13 planet's total. Pluto, just found in 1930, leaves much to learn. There is talk of a new planet even today, but nothing is firm yet. In addition the other 8 planets can ASPECT each other. This infers to (effects, uplift, uproot, upset or actuate) each other. An aspect can do so to Jupiter at different points around the map's circle. This can change Jupiter a great deal. Generally what I have shown you will prevail.

Now in looking at Saturn as it transit's (or moves from year to year) in an anti-clockwise motion, it will INDICATE your success greatly. This is the planet that indicates you can do no wrong, or you can do nothing right. Saturn can indicate your at the head of the list when it peaks at D. From A to B with Saturn, you can't buy a break anywhere. Getting ahead is impossible and you just as well relax and secure what you have. From B to C. Saturn is a little more kind in that it indicates people notice you. Competition is still mighty rough. Then from C to A Saturn indicates your the winner. Few can get ahead of you in the fish bowl.

The peak is at D that is the 10th house you will notice. Good advice is when Saturn reaches the 11th house start your program of securing your success. If you don't try to gain more ground into the 11th house and secure your success right up to A you should be able to keep your gains right on despite A to B. Of course if you have crossed over the line of honesty in your gains you will likely lose all of them no matter what. If your gains have been for the wrong reasons you will most likely lose them too. If you try to gain from the 11th house on you will most likely lost all of your gains, which will make the time from A to B very hard to take because you will have nothing. Take a look at O. J. Simpson.

Saturn moves much slower than Jupiter and takes 29 years to go completely around the map. See my simplified GRAPH charts in FIGURE 9

A good example of both Jupiter and Saturn peaking together (GRAPH CHART 9) in the fish bowl area is the child stars in the movies. When they get older, you never see them any more. A to B gets them. When both Jupiter and Saturn travel A to B

(GRAPH CHART 9 at the same time you will have illness. Depression to a point of the need of hospital care can happen. If you should experience Saturn at D—E while Jupiter is at A—B (GRAPH CHART 9) you find your negative outlook will cost you any breaks you could have had. Should Jupiter be at D—E while Saturn is at A—B, (GRAPH CHART 9) then you just can't understand. You feel you should have been successful. You could never get a chance. Now you know why the other guy got the promotion. His Saturn and Jupiter were higher than yours in that old fish bowl. It was not that he was better than you

*James W. Nichols*

19          19                  19

82 83 84 85 86 87 88 89 90 91 92 93 94 95 96 97 98 99 0

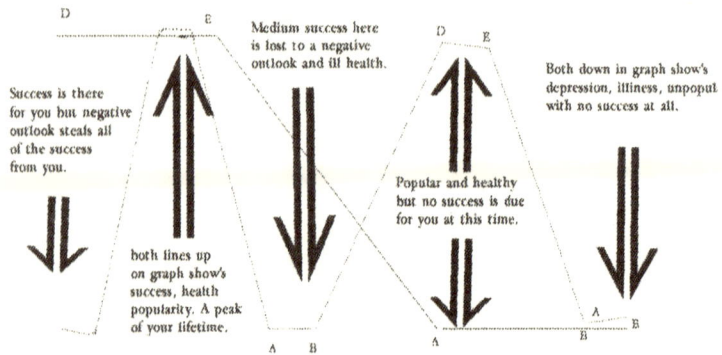

SATURN SHOW'S SUCCESS OR NO SUCCESS.

JUPITER SHOW'S POSITIVE OR NEGATIVE OUTLOOK. ALSO SHOW'S POPULAR OR UNPOPULAR.

**FIGURE 9**

it was just his time to succeed. I use to think it was something I had not done. Then, I read about it, in Grant Lewi's books.

Mars is your energy drive indicator and works about the same in A—B. Low energy. An increase in energy comes right away when Mars reaches past B. From D to E your Mars indicates you full of energy. Of course Mars can be strong or weak in your Natal (frozen) map. How much energy we have in our life depends on Mars strength. Some people we call Workaholic's have a mars indication of extreme strength in there frozen map.

You must remember that where the frozen (NATAL) planets locate in your Natal (frozen) map will indicate how much total energy you will ever have. How much total positive outlook you will ever have. How much total popularity you will ever have, and the total of your success height you can ever reach.

I suggest some good TRANSIT books (after you're into astrology), written by Frances Sakoian and Louis Acker. They are easy to read too. The titles are, Transit's of Jupiter, Transit's of Mars, Transit's of Saturn, Transit's of Uranus, Transit's of Neptune, Transit's of Pluto.

These books and Grant Lewi's books helped me to understand my Fathers chart. I could never figure out how Dad could enter into the flying business in 1920 and continue to be successful right up to 1942. We had the big depression in 1929 and many businesses went completely under.

Even many of the company's who build airplanes went out of business during that period. My Dad however built a garage to repair auto's for a back up job, built a hanger for one plane and borrowed $3,000.00 to buy his second plane in about 1930. We did not even own a home. We rented, but never missed a meal, had proper clothes and people of the upper class (with money), came to Dad to learn to fly.

Everyone wanted an airplane of their own after they learned to fly, so Dad sold them airplanes. My Dad was an honest man. He never took advantage of anyone. As a result his good fortune carried on for him up till World War 2 in 1942. His lifestyle changed but he kept his money because of his good outlook and honesty.

The US Government wanted Dad's Tri-Motor Ford in 1942 and insisted on the sale. This put him out of the flying business for good. He kept all he had secured in the fish bowl of success and purchased a farm. We were able to maintain a normal life there, but Dad never made an abundance of money. He plugged along working hard, and being happy just working for himself.

When his Transit Jupiter and Saturn cycled to the fish bowl area again, Dad made one purchase of another farm. It was double the size of the old one, for the same money as the old one. He then became popular again, made money farming, buying more equipment. By the time he passed on in 1975 his estate was worth about $300,000. My poor step mother managed to manipulate most of the money into her accounts for the week he was in the hospital. It did her little good. She went almost blind and didn't trust anyone at all. She worried someone would take her money till the day she died. You can't be greedy and win. You will lose every time.

Many people tried to haul airplane passengers from Port Columbus, but could never make a go of it prior to 1930. Dad went there and stayed at Port Columbus, from 1934 to 1942. He charged 60 cents for a ride in his plane.

These things are just some of the proofs you see when you do Astrology. No wonder people get hooked when they see how systematic the science is.

Ever notice how movie stars go overseas to another country when their popularity starts to drop here in the USA? They do you know. If you look into it you will see most of them do this. Could it be they got the information from an Astrologer that while they are unpopular in the USA, in Europe they are popular? You can bet on it folks. Moving around on our planet changes our maps. If you know to move at the right time, to the right place, you can keep your planets in the fish bowl the whole time, but you have to move on to the other side of the planet 180 degrees.

The BEE GEE'S singing group showed up on TV from the 1970 period just this week. They were a big hit overseas for years. Then they returned to the USA, and immediately received a spot on TV. What timing that was. It was not by accident. Somewhere an Astrologer was at work for them.

Did you realize that some Natal (frozen) charts would tell if the person is:

Prone to having affairs with the opposite sex

Has a suicide tendency

That they are of no morals

You can see that they are good salesman

Full of musical talent or no musical talent

You can see them as lazy or a workaholic

If they are reliable, unreliable, truthful or very much a liar.

When your marriage will be tested

When you should not sign papers of any kind

When you should start projects

When you will have more than one marriage

When you will need courage in your life

When you should buy a car and when not to

When to buy a home or not to buy a home

When to have children and when not to.

When Astrologer does a Natal (frozen) chart for two people he can tell them how well they get along:

If they should get married or not

If their attraction is only sexual

If they complement each other or not

When and if they should have children, so they will fit into the family and feel comfortable, not like outcasts.

Most Astrologers only give you what you ask for in the way of information. It is a lot of work to look up everything. When your work will change, or if it will remain the same for several years. When money will come your way, when you will be lucky, or perhaps you were born very lucky.

Astrologers can see love at first sight between two people, and it does happen. My last wife and I had that experience. Both of us were from multiple marriages. Both of us swore not to get married again. We would not date because neither wanted any more relationships. Finally after many months of seeing and just speaking to each other, we went out. It was so enjoyable to be together, we didn't date, just hung out with each other. I did her chart for her when she found out I was into Astrology. I could not believe this woman. Everything about her was very pleasing to me.

I still could not see our ever being more than friends because there was 19 year's difference in our ages. To much to ask for, wouldn't you say! I tried to stay away from her for a couple of months. She missed me, and I missed her. We both got married after about a year and have never had one cross word, agree on every thing. Both have our mood's compatible with each other. During our five years together, she expressed her confusion about a dream she had repeatedly as a little girl. She dreamed of an all white room with a view where she could see beautiful roses down a driveway. She had ask everyone about this dream. When she described the dream to me, tears ran down my cheeks.

My mother, I told you about earlier, who died at 46, in a sudden death auto accident, had a favorite room upstairs in our old farm house. The room was all white, and she sat at the window hour after hour looking out at her roses along our drive way. By the way my wife is very tense riding in cars. Spirit's do come back to be with loved ones. Sometimes they carry hidden memories from past lives with them. In reviewing my wife's natal (frozen) map, and my natal (frozen) map, I found 14 points of attraction between us. We both have the ability to overlook and forget anything the other might do. As one final test I ask what else she remembered in her childhood dreams. She described a room with a desk and a telephone. She said it was a funny shaped phone. She had never seen one like it before.

I drew a picture of the old style phone we had at our farm house in 1945 before she was ever born in 1949. That did it for both of us. We never talk about it, but down deep we know. Like the book by Dick Sutphen, "YOU WERE BORN AGAIN TO BE TOGETHER." (1976 printing.

I failed the sixth grade. It was a bad year in my life. When I did my personal natal (frozen) map in 1968, the year I failed was the first thing I checked out. Both Saturn and Jupiter hit the bottom that year for me. I also noticed in my natal (frozen) map when I was two years of age, both Saturn and Jupiter were at a peak in my fish bowl.

I could never figure out what this does for a little two year old kid. Then, while visiting an 84 year old friend of the family, she dug out her scrap book. She showed me my baby picture in the newspaper. I had won a baby contest at two years of age, so you see it works. Young or old, it works. Even if your dead it works, because your name comes into the fish bowl. How many actors, novelists, musicians have you heard honored even after they have passed away? Elvis is a good example.

I have gone over many chart's of accidents. A needed precise timing in an accident pulls everyone together. All of the participating people need to be at that one spot at the same time. People say it was his unlucky day! Planning is a big part of our lifetime test's. A good friend told me from his hospital bed how he changed his mind suddenly in advance of a trip to work. It cost him ten weeks in the hospital and he has never gone back to work since. All he did was change his normal route. He met a guy who went to sleep and ran him off the road on that new route that morning.

When I got out of the Air Force after four years in Korea, I didn't have a dime, and found a job in construction. I was out of town near Akron, renting a room in an old man's house. We all socialized during the evenings, other guys renting rooms, my self, and the old man. He played any instrument he touched, with no lessons at all. I had never seen a THERMION before. It's a very old German electrical instrument operated by body capacity. You don't touch it, just put your hands near it for different notes. He could play any tune you could name. He also could play a saw. He was very, very gifted.

He had asked everyone their birthdays when we came for rooms. I noticed he told two guys he was full, and I knew he had three more rooms. He and I talked one evening under the moon on his fount porch. In my outward way, I ask why he turned them away like that. He said astrology showed them as bad people and he did not want them around. He then proceeded to tell me how hard my last 7 years had been. He assured me that night, in 6 years I would be the president of a large construction company. I laughed, as anyone would. During the next two weeks I was there, I noticed his room lined with books, most of which were Astrology books.

I forgot all about the old man until that day. The company I worked for called me to their office. The announcement, I was to be their new president. He was right there with me that day, in spirit. I think he is still with me. Someone is telling me what to say, because I am not that smart. All I have ever asked for is the truth, never anything else. Now that I have it, no one wants to hear it from me.

The new job promotion required me to move to Chicago from Cleveland Ohio. I told my wife to look for a place to rent until we could feel this job out for a couple of years. Also we could get to know the city and see where we would like to live. After two months of my working night and day, the wife advised me she liked only one house. The house was only for sale. She liked nothing she saw for rent. I gave in, against my instinct, and it was a very bad mistake. When I left the company 2 years later, the house market had dropped. Any money accumulated I lost in selling the house, and moving back to Ohio.

It was during this period that I began to wonder, what I had done wrong. With almost 12 years of hard work, I was back at zero, with no future in view. I first turned to religion, as many people do, who are down, and lost have faith. That helped, but I kept studying hard and finding problems with my teachers who could not answer my Bible questions. In religion, you don't ask questions. Just act on faith. I read, I studied, and became a big time Bible pusher. This lost me almost every friend I knew. No one likes a **Do-GOOD'ER BIBLE PERSON**.

Religion and my faith almost cost me my marriage when I gave $2000.00 to a PREACHER for his radio school. I followed preacher after preacher, from one church to six others trying to get answers and learn. Every man let me down. In 1968, I sat in my basement study room and ask GOD to please give me the truth. Mixed messages from mixed preachers confused me badly. God and his blessed spirit lead the right into Astrology in the Bible.

My marriage test (which all marriages have at one time or another), failed badly. Even after 21 years. It was destiny that it falls apart.

Another quick 7 year marriage and I said that's all! I settled down in a little apartment broke. Worked and read and did Astrology charts. That was the extent of my life. I even did a chart for the lady who rented me my apartment. As is usual, I did not hear from her for a few weeks. My truth charts effect people that way I guess. Then one night, she called and raved about my charts. Said I was the only person who had ever opened her life for her to see. We became friends and she helped me make my charts easier to read. I applied for a job that would require about 16 hours a day and had no thoughts of marriage despite my attraction to this lady. Both of us married before were gun shy of any type of affair. When I did not get the big job, I then had time for a wife, and we got married. We are so happy with our 14 heavy points of attraction.

It was all there in our charts and easy to see when I had eyes to see. We tend to only hear and see what we desire to see and hear, without even knowing it. We ignore what is right in front of our noses. It's hard to learn to open your mind and learn to except truth. You must tune into your spirit and follow that wonderful soul. Every answer you need will come to you. It makes your life more sensible and reasonable. Books that lack truth just turn me off, even today, after all of these years.

Your Natal (frozen) map will indicate if you will ever be a leader, a follower, rich, medium rich, or poor. The (MOVING) planets transit through that NATAL map, and what they will indicate is also aspected by their location in the natal frozen blueprint at your first breath. Aspects are degrees of respect between Planets (frozen) in the natal chart, and Transit Planets (moving) in the (frozen) natal chart.

Reviewing charts of your own life time is very informative, but reviewing charts of other's life times is even more informative.

In doing many Doctors maps I notice they are gifted and indicated to be a Doctor. Of course there are a few that just pass the test due to a strong brain indication. Bad news if you get one of those.

I had a Doctor who became a close friend. I tried so hard to show him the value of Astrology to diagnose an illness. He just would not engage in any of it despite our close friendship. His wife, believed and read, and like myself, saw the value. I moved away and was 3 states distant when I received a letter from the Doctors wife. The Doctor was ill and no one could diagnose what was wrong. This was 1979. I looked up the Doctor's astrological records and spent a week or more on them. Finally I wrote the wife and advised her that he could not fight off germs. He required full isolation protection. The planet Uranus (a major planet in our lives) gave me this indication from his map. Two years later she wrote and thanked me. I had been correct in the diagnose, according to the attending Doctors. It was fatal and she just returned from the funeral. I think about the Doctor a lot these days as I listen to the stories of AIDS. It scares me a lot. He was such a good person.

I have been working on a system to use Astrology to make determinations of the weather. Those accomplished years ago, dropped from the written word. So far I find that my forecasts are very localized, within a 25 mile radius. I have a system to tell me when it will snow or rain within about 2 hours, but the temperature determinations are still a bit hard for me yet. Perhaps if I live long enough I will get it worked out and maybe write about it.

I have a feeling that the microwave signals, which are just thick today, as well as the high tension wires, could vary the magnetic flux in areas to a point that would change forecasts. Columbus Ohio has a dividing line in weather north of (I-70 and south of same. Study shows this line really works too. To fly over I-70 you notice right off, all of the towers of microwave transmitters that follow along I-70. THINK ABOUT THAT FRIENDS.

The USSR and the USA can move weather using alternating waves. The problem is these waves work only on the opposite side of the earth, from the transmitted location, according to the books I have read. If Mr. Tesla were alive, he would have had this system all worked out by now easy. I did Tesla's birth map, July 10, 1856, and this man was truly gifted. The word GENIUS truly fit this man. It is such a pity our history books don't tell the younger generation about him. Margaret Cheney did write a book, "TESLA" (man out of time), in 1981. It is the best book by far and had many details about him.

I mentioned a chart earlier I will explain now for you. If you look at FIGURE 5 you will see how I keep track of what to do and when, regarding the moon and living things. Most calendars have the moon signs written on them now days. A more detailed book with the dates worked out for you in advance is the LLEWELYN'S MOON SIGN BOOK. It costs about five dollars or so from Llewellyn Publications P.O. Box 64383 St. Paul, Mn 55164-0383. Almost all of the books I mention you may purchase from this distrtibutor.

Number's in the Bible keep repeating. There are 12's, 7's, 3's, 4's, and on and on. One number is confusing to everyone that is the number 144,000 in revelations. Well folks if you take,

the number of houses in a natal map,

the number of planets the Bible speaks of (13),

the number of possible aspects,

the three divisions of each house,

Multiple them all together, it comes out close to 144,467. I must add that science is now finding that our bodies have some where in the area of 140,000 genes also. That is not just a coincidence in my opinion. God is good at math, don't you think so?

Benjamin Franklin wrote an article "THE ANATOMY OF MAN'S BODY AS GOVERNED BY THE TWELVE CONSTELLATIONS" in 1753. He wrote how to secure your building from lightning flashes.  He truly understood nature and GOD.

The very cells of your body and mind determine the degree of quality of the individual.  WE must be consistent with the corporeal demands of the larger body parts.  The peculiar type of cell that makes up human flesh is a different degree in density than the physical cells of a fish, or a tree, or even a rock.

Remember physical matter is to suit the need for your life experience.  In some instances we have seen people deformed.  I know that this deformity is for a reason.  It has to due with a life lesson for them or someone around them or maybe even KARMA, (judgment from another life time).

Reincarnation tells me an Entity sent to the earth's magnetic sphere comes for a need of some kind.  It will continue to come down until appeased or you commit suicide like a damn fool.

A person may struggle through a lifetime without arrival at success AS THE WORLD KNOWS IT.    Another person produces abundantly by sheer instinct, without the labor of even thinking.  This is a true child of good fortune.  THE WORLD then condemns one as a failure, the other as a genius.  The first has made true visions by his effort.  The second has done no more than have the knowing of a full soul.  The measure of progress, is not always the work of the hand, or the mouth, but the inner fashion of each one's soul.

A true story about Tesla I must share with you.  It seems the US Government got mad at Tesla for some reason.  They said they would take him into court.  Tesla then drove two stakes into the earth at his lab in Colorado, ran wires to the stakes from his lab and told the Government, if they took him to court he would reverse the poles of our planet.  The North pole becomes the south pole and visa-versa.  If this happens nothing would run anywhere in the world. It shook up the USA so much they dropped the argument and nothing came of it again. So you see, Tesla was a genius, EVEN IN THE EYES OF OUR OWN GOVERNMENT. The Government confiscated all his equipment and notes at his death. They must fear someone else might try the same thing.

This A.M. I watched the wild fires in California on TV. I wondered if the people there would have listened if someone had warned them of that coming devastation. Only those who have ears will hear. I am sure that ASTROLOGY studies of California would have indicated the fires. Astrology studies of the Mississippi area would have indicated the big floods. I feel sure that Astrology studies of earth quakes would pin point times and places. There are not enough people working on this science, or even looking at it. Like others of the world, most Astrologers work only for MONEY. I am sure that many of the world problems are solvable if more people HAD EARS TO HEAR, EYES TO SEE AND USED THEIR SOUL TO FEEL.

Then there is the Mayan people who were experts at Astrology according to records found in their ruins. They just disappeared from the earth. Are we about to disappear from the earth with all of our knowledge we have gained? We don't except Astrology, so we are still safe for a while.

MAY THOSE WHO HAVE EARS.....HEAR!

MAY THOSE WHO HAVE EYES.....SEE!

AMEN

PLEASE READ FOR YOURSELF. DON'T SIT AND LISTEN TO OTHERS TELL YOU WHAT TO BELIEVE. Here are some more books that are very good.

Anything written by Joan McEvers on Astrology is good reading. The Book of Macrobiotics by Michio Kushi Japan Publications, Inc. is good. "Life Forces" by Louis Stewart Universal Press is also good. Write me, I will give you any list's you want, books, Bibles. I would love to hear from you. I answer all letters.

You must read Sydney Omarr's book ANSWER IN THE SKY....Almost.

Thank you Sydney for having the guts to say the truth!

> Jim Nichols
> 9350 E. Speedway #21
> Tucson, Az 85710-1838

The pages following this last page of my book are a complementary copy of my birth chart as I have arranged it with the graphs I have described earlier. Note the (Read A or B or C) notes that show aspects of major planets. In addition to this graph system I have enclosed a copy of my mood chart for myself to show you how it works and looks. This is the same system I have given earlier as a disk for you to compute your own moods. Please note all of these systems are under copyright to me and without written permission you may not use them.

THESE ARE INSTRUCTIONS ON HOW TO READ THE
GRAPH MAP OF YOUR LIFE FROM BIRTH TO THE YEAR
2049. SEE GRAPH MAP'S AFTER THESE INSTRUCTIONS.

THE GREEN LINE ON YOUR GAPH MAP shows your
SUCCESS in life as very easy or very hard. The upper half of
the graph is considered as positive and would be easy success.
The lower half of the graph is considered as negative and would
be hard. The further up in the upper half the line is the easier
success is. The further down in the lower half the harder success
is. What you have accumulated in success while the line is in the
upper half of your chart you may keep generally while the line is
going back through the lower half. You must stop expanding
and becoming more successful before the line enters the lower
half on its way down. If you continue to grow more successful
below the half way point on the way down you will most likely
loose everything you have gained during your success period
when the green line hits the bottom of the chart. This can many
times include your marriage if it is started while the green line is
in the lower half of your graph. So I advise you to only consider
marriage when the green line is up off of the bottom of the graph
going in an up-ward direction.

THE RED LINE ON YOUR GRAPH MAP shows your
MENTAL OUTLOOK on life and indicates you think positive or
you think negative. The top half of the graph is considered as
positive and would make you think very positive about all things
and have faith in everything you do. The bottom half of the
graph is considered as negative and would make you think very
negative about all things and have no faith in anything you might
do or that others might do. When your line is positive you attract
others who are positive who help you. When your line is

negative you attract others who are negative and will drag you down even further into negative thinking.

WHEN BOTH RED AND GREEN LINES ARE IN UPPER HALF OF YOUR GRAPH you will be in a peak of your life period having huge success, and many good friends will help you.

WHEN BOTH RED AND GREEN LINES ARE ON THE VERY BOTTOM OF YOUR GRAPH you will be very depressed with possible illness and almost no friends. If this happens in your teen years you may become a drop out and not finish school at all. I have Cassette tapes to help you during this period by hypnosis. In 30's to 40's this will be your change of life period. This is also a period ripe for divorce, business failure and the like.

WHEN YOUR GREEN SUCCESS LINE IS IN THE UPPER HALF OF YOUR GRAPH AND YOUR RED MENTAL LINE IS ON THE VERY BOTTOM OF THE GRAPH you will over look any success because of your negative outlook and bad friends. Your success is wasted away.

WHEN YOUR GREEN SUCCESS LINE IS ON THE VERY BOTTOM OF YOUR GRAPH AND YOUR RED MENTAL LINE IS IN THE UPPER HALF OF YOUR GRAPH you will feel you can do anything, and will have good friends, but you will not be allowed to succeed despite all of your efforts or your friends efforts to help you. It is a good time to relax, study and learn. Marriage during this period will fail generally as will business expansion. Don't gamble during this period.

When a year is marked (A), (B), or (C) go to the back three pages which are marked A, B, and C. Find the paragraph with the year marked on it and read. This will give additional information for that years outlook.

If your birth time is off by 4 minutes your chart may vary by a year or more. You can adjust the graph lines to be more suited to your life problems if you feel the need by moving all of the year indicators left or all of the year indicators right.

for your entertainment only

James W. Nichols

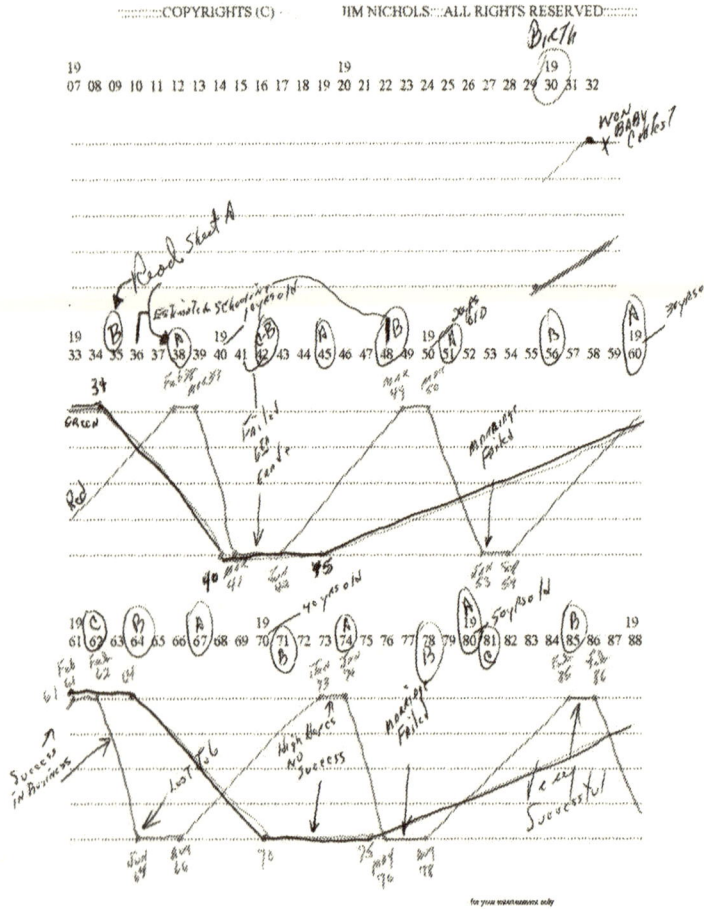

90

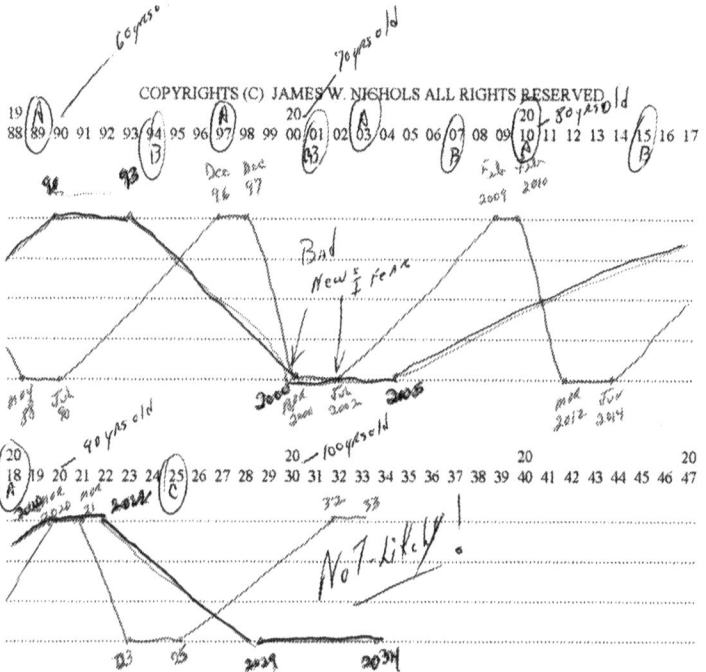

# TO BE USED WITH THE GRAPH LIFE CHART

## Aspect of Saturn toward Saturn A-SHEET

When your planet Saturn aspects a lower square to itself on the dates listed below choices will be made. If these choices are wise you will receive accomplishments in 7 years so think out your choices wisely.

1938-1967-1997

..................................................................................

When your planet Saturn aspects an opposition to itself on the dates listed below our personality changes, ego satisfaction is required, and your personality can recede into itself or become extroverted for the world to see. This happens two times in most life times. Around ages 13 and 16 and again about 40 to 45. Your choice at the early date will result in either good or bad mental and material results according to the choice, wise of foolish. During the second date you will feel a turning point in your career.

1945-1974-2003

..................................................................................

When your planet Saturn aspects as upper square to itself on the dates listed below you will find yourself revising your aims in life or business. Maybe even dumping some of the dead wood in your life. Most likely it needed thinning out anyway in your opinion at least.

1951-1980-2010

..................................................................

When your planet Saturn returns to the place of your birth on the dates listed below you will see a shift in human relations. Marriage, or divorce, or change of jobs, leaving home, moving etc.

1960-1989-2018

..................................................................

for your entertainment only

# TO BE USED WITH THE GRAPH LIFE CHART.

## SAT-SUN B-SHEET

Lower square will happen in            1935-1964-1994-2023

....................................................................

These years mark new starts in your life.  New obligations. Breaking old ties.  Leaving home.  Starting a career.  Marriage or business break.  Don't expect miracles.  Go slow for it takes some time.

Opposition will happen in            1942-1971-2001

....................................................................

These years are very difficult.  Your temperamental, feel abused, low on vitality.  Quarrels, separations, ill health but afterwards you will feel very knowledgeable.  Make yourself the type of person you want to be and you will have a happy ending.

Upper square will happen in            1948-1979-2007

....................................................................

These years are a high point in prestige or the collapse of your hopes.  Aim again if you've failed.  Be more objective. Go for something you can do.

Conjunct will happen in            1956-1985-2015

....................................................................

These years are the results of your past at a climax. Did you get get a crown of achievement or did you go in the wrong direction and finish last? If your successful don't let it go to your head. If your down the tube try again in a new direction.

for your entertainment only

# TO BE USED WITH THE GRAPH LIFE CHART

## URA-SUN aspects C-SHEET

A lower square will happen in the years          2001

...............................................................

Unsettled domestic affairs, rebellion, temperament rules you now.  If you rule it, you can grow.  Alterations and changes, make them and move on.

An opposition will happen in the years          1942-2026

...............................................................

Breaking of old ties and the making of new ones.  Its not a good time for getting married, so forget it.  Nerves, impulses, self-indulgence, and don't force others now.  Let them figure it out for themselves.

An upper square will happen in the years          1962

...............................................................

Shift in worldly status.  Change in job.  Sudden events.  Use self-controlled temperament to gain.

A conjunct will happen in the years          1981

...............................................................

There will be sudden changes in your attitude toward life and yourself.  You will become in spokesperson and you will win support from many.  Dreams come true, inner peace, accomplishment, satisfaction or....it could be a nightmare, defeat, inadequacy if in the past you did not believe in yourself. Watch for new opportunities and forge ahead.

for your entertainment only

# THE HUMAN MOOD CHART BY DATE AND TIME FOR EACH DAY OF THE MONTH

### For your entertainment only

The human body is about 70% salt water, just as the surface of the earth is 70% covered with salt water. For this reason I feel our bodies are influenced by the moon changes, shape, location, etc. just as the oceans are, by a tidal movement. In people it changes their moods. In oceans it changes the elevation of the shore waters. It is my opinion that the electrical system of our bodies is effected by this movement of salt water within us, and therefore the mood changes. While I cannot provide scientific proof I can give you charts that will support me by showing you, your moods, and those of loved ones, months and years ahead of having these moods. They have been very effective for students in taking tests at certain times. It could be effective for Airline Pilot's, Bus Drivers, and those related to other peoples lives, if I could only show them these charts. So far only ONE Airline has used my charts. To explain these moods as given on my charts for you.

The day of the month on the outside of the circle starts with 1st up to the 30th or 31st and will be read around the circle opposite the direction of a clock.

The start of a FUN PERIOD (right side) runs until the end of FUN PERIOD (left side). In the upper middle of this period is the PEAK MENTAL PERIOD. The fun period is a time of joy, funny things, laughter, enjoyment of your friends. A time when your thinking is sharp. You will make good judgments, do well on tests etc. At the peak mental you can pass any test (if you studied for it) and you are a little independent, taking or leaving sex as you see fit.

The FOUR POOR HOURS happen just before the start of the fun period (right side) and just after the fun period ends (on left side). The four poor hours are a time of bad news, up-set stomach, nightmares, worry, mental confusion, PMS in females, accidents, you may drop things, or loose things. Should the 4 poor hours happen during a date near the full moon they will be harder to take and will jump ahead in time by almost 12 hours. If they happen during a new moon they will be lighter and easier to take. I have not determined why just yet, but watch for this in your charts. The NEW or FULL moon must happen right on or within a few hours of your date I have listed to effect the time changing for you. I have tried to give the time range beginning to end as close as I can.

Right after you leave your 4 poor hours (left side) you will enter your SYMPATHETIC PERIOD. This will run until just before your next 4 poor hour period (right side). In your sympathetic period your will cry for any reason, movies, hurt feelings, memories, a look, a word, just anything can set you off. Gifts means so much now. Flowers can mean as much as a large gift because you are so tuned into sympathy. Sex is very strong now and females are very strong to conceive children during this period. In the middle of this sympathetic period you will have the BORED PERIOD (bottom) during which you just go from one thing to another and can find nothing to keep your mind happy.

These charts are perfect for mothers to explain why the child is acting as they are. Why your husband is the way he is, and should a husband and wife have their 4 poor hours at the same time they could feel like a divorce is needed about two times per month. By separating from each other during the 4 poor hours they will be very happy with one another, but they need to know when the times are for the 4 poor hours.

If you desire additional charts later on, please let me know if the time was off for your 4 poor hour periods. I can adjust accordingly for further charts and make them right on time for you.

for your entertainment only

# MOOD CHART FOR
# MONTH OF March-1996 ONLY

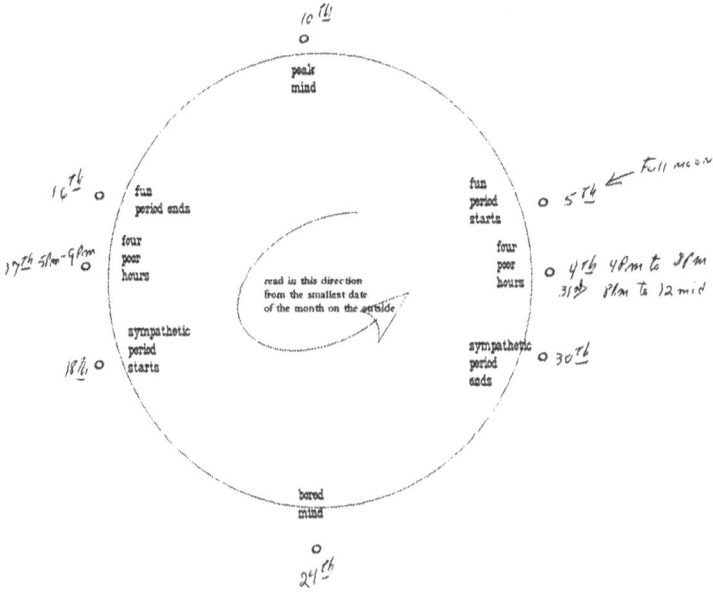

# ABOUT THE AUTHOR

Seventy years of living, reading, learning from my own errors and the errors of others around me gave me the effort to write this book. My experiences and the experiences of others I have helped have proven beyond a doubt the facts included in this book. My only desire is to ease the pain of life with understanding and I have put it into graph form for ease of understanding.

A common man writes this book for all other common people in common language because you should share in this understanding. This is not a Bible book, nor am I pushing any religion, but you will surely agree after reading it that there is a higher order somewhere in charge of our lives.